Unmasking Japan

Unmasking Japan

Myths and Realities About
the Emotions of the Japanese

David Matsumoto

Stanford University Press
Stanford, California
1996

Stanford University Press
Stanford, California
© 1996 by the Board of Trustees of the
Leland Stanford Junior University
Printed in the United States of America

CIP data appear at the end of the book

Stanford University Press publications are distributed exclusively by
Stanford University Press within the United States, Canada, Mexico, and
Central America; they are distributed exclusively by Cambridge University
Press throughout the rest of the world.

For Nobuko

9

Acknowledgments

The studies and ideas presented in this book have never been solely my own. Rather, they represent the culmination of many different collaborative efforts with many different researchers, agencies, and institutions over the past decade, and therefore they are as much a product of cooperative efforts in the enterprise of scholarship as they are my own. Although the people who have helped in our research program over the years are too numerous to mention, I wish to single out a few who have played a key role in the conduct of the studies reported.

Paul Ekman, professor of psychology, University of California, San Francisco, has been a mentor, research supervisor, teacher, colleague, and friend. Our relationship has spanned over a decade, during which time he has taught me the intricacies of human emotion and facial expressions. A world-renowned leader of research and theorizing in the field of human emotion, Dr. Ekman inspired in me the excitement of doing research in the field, especially in examining how cultures shaped and molded facial expressions and emotional experience. His work has been, and continues to be, an inspiration to my own thinking.

Wally Friesen, adjunct professor, University of California, San Francisco, has also been a mentor, colleague, and friend. During my stay at his (and Ekman's) laboratory during the early 1980s, Wally was instrumental in teaching me many of the nuts and bolts of doing research, introducing me to computers, databases, and data analyses. His encouragement of my own inquiry into culture and emotion always played in the back of my mind, as my cross-cultural research program on emotion grew.

Klaus Scherer, professor of psychology, University of Geneva, Switzerland, and Harald Wallbott, adjunct professor, University of Giessen, Germany, were the primary investigators of our studies on the antecedents of and reactions to emotion in Japan. Our research on Japan on these topics was part of a larger research project that involved over 30 different countries with 3,000 respondents on five different continents, and the help we received from Professors Scherer and Wallbott was invaluable in the collection of these data in Japan and in the subsequent development of different ideas about culture and emotion.

Tsutomu Kudoh, professor of psychology, Osaka University of Education, Japan, has been instrumental in the design, conduct, and interpretation of all the research reported in this book. Professor Kudoh has been an invaluable co-investigator for our research program in Japan, and it has been my pleasure to continue a collaboration that began in the early 1980s when Professor Kudoh was a Visiting Scholar at Ekman and Friesen's laboratory. We collaborated on the translation of one of Ekman and Friesen's books, *Unmasking the Face*, and we also worked together on the subject of cultural differences as revealed in body postures. The present book is only the most recent of many different projects in which we have helped each other in our respective research programs. Without Professor Kudoh's help, we would never have been able to amass the wealth of information we have on the emotions in Japan. This book is as much his as it is mine.

Over the years, my research laboratories at San Francisco State University and earlier at the Wright Institute and the University of California, Berkeley, have benefited from the participation of many undergraduate and graduate research assistants. Among the many, I should like to give my thanks to the person who has done more than anyone else to aid my research program in Japan. I first met Masami Kobayashi at UC Berkeley, where she was an undergraduate psychology student. Wishing to become involved with research, she aided me in the collection of the data of some of our judgment studies comparing American and Japanese responses to faces. Since then, she has been an invaluable aid in all my cross-cultural research in Japan. Much of the research reported in this book is the result of her support and activities over the years as a research assistant in my laboratory.

A number of agencies and institutions have provided support for the various research projects reported in this book. Much of our research on the emotions in Japan was supported in part by a research grant from the National Institute of Mental Health (MH 42749-01), and an American Psychological Association Minority Fellowship under Clinical Training Grant 5 T01 MH13833 from the National Institute of Mental Health. Our research has also been supported by a Research Fellowship from the Wright Institute (1986–1989), and by President's Research and Professional Development Grants, Affirmative Action Awards, and California State University Awards for Research, Scholarship, and Professional Activity from San Francisco State University (1989–1992).

I am also grateful for the support I have received from my editors at Stanford University Press—Muriel Bell and John Feneron, and the copy editor, Shirley Taylor. I am very pleased to have placed this book with Stanford, to add to their impressive line of books in the area of Japanese studies.

My family has made many sacrifices over the years, not only in the production of this monograph but also during the conduct of the many studies on which this book is based. I have had to devote many early mornings and late evenings to work at the computer, telephone, or fax machine, and the nature of the research has also meant extensive travel. This book is as much a product of the efforts and sacrifices of my family, and especially my wife, Nobuko, without whose patience and understanding none of this could have occurred.

Finally, I should like to express my deep appreciation to the thousands of people, in the United States and Japan and elsewhere, who have participated in our research program as subject participants. Without their cooperation, we would never have been able to uncover new information about the feelings and emotions of people the world over. It is to them, the respondents in our many studies, that I offer my final words of gratitude.

D. M.

Contents

Figures

Preface

Japan has long held the fascination of scholars and laypeople alike. Our interest, and to some extent need, to understand the Japanese culture and its people is greater today than ever before. The last twenty years in particular have been witness to growth in interest and fascination with the Japanese, and the emergence of Japan as a world economic power has stimulated many works that have attempted to understand the Japanese from the point of view of differences in work ethic and managerial styles. Scholarly works, however, have focused on the Japanese culture and its people, many of them having developed into excellent resources on Japan and the Japanese. This book follows in this tradition, with this underlying philosophy: in order to understand a nation, one must first understand the culture underlying that nation; in order to understand the culture, one must understand the psychology of the people constituting that culture.

Many books share this philosophy, some of which have become standard texts in the field. The works by Condon (1984) and Hall (1976), for example, present a good, basic introduction to Japanese culture. Condon and Saito's (1974) edited volume contains several interesting and provocative chapters on intercultural communication with the Japanese, and Barnlund's (1975) book presents many more in detail. Several more scientifically oriented resources representing psychological (e.g., Doi, 1973), sociological (e.g., Nakane, 1970), and anthropological (e.g., Lebra, 1976; Benedict, 1946) points of view also exist. More comprehensive, scholarly works on Japanese society are also available, notably those by Reischauer (1988), Dore (1967), and Vogel (1963).

The present work, though it shares some of the philosophy of the previous books, differs in certain key ways. These include:

1. *A focus on the Japanese as people.* The focus of the book is not on Japanese culture or society per se; rather, it is on how Japanese culture and society structure, shape, and mold the emotions of the Japanese people. All cultures shape and mold emotions, but the degree to which the Japanese culture shapes emotion has led to several misunderstandings about the emotional life of the Japanese, which this book attempts to correct.

2. *A focus on human emotions.* The bulk of the book is focused on various aspects of human emotion in Japanese life. Emotion, being a language and a topic that all people can understand, is the most appropriate vehicle for bridging the gap between people of different cultures. This book presents the Japanese as human beings with real feelings and emotions rather than as mindless pawns caught in the web of their own culture.

Over the years, the topic of emotions in the Japanese has received considerable attention. Benedict (1946) characterized the Japanese culture as a shame culture, emphasizing the importance of this emotion in the lives of the Japanese, but several writers since then have countered her theories about the importance of shame and the absence of guilt, citing the importance of both emotions in the lives of the individual Japanese within society (e.g., Lebra, Doi). Lebra (1976) also focused some attention on other emotions and emotional processes, such as love, hate, sex, and empathy. Doi (1973, 1985) characterized his work on *amae* as a study of human emotion in Japan.

Despite these works, the importance of emotions in Japan is often overlooked or underplayed by Japan scholars. One of the reasons for this has been the fact that emotions are often considered extraneous to scholarly investigation and seemingly unworthy of scientific examination. Until recently, there have been very few studies of emotion in Japan as a valid and important variable in itself. All these factors have contributed to our inability to make a crucial and generalizable link between our theoretical, abstract understanding of culture and society to meaningful, and universal, emotional events on the level of the individual Japanese.

The comparative study of emotions in Japan serves this purpose well and fills a major gap in our understanding of the Japanese. Given our theoretical understanding of Japanese culture and society, we are now better able than before to link culture with individual behavior and emotions. Owing in part to the advancement in our methods of examining emotions scientifically, the study of emotion has gained considerable standing in the scholarly community, and in the last two decades, systematic research on emotion in Japan blending these two streams has produced a substantial body of knowledge about Japanese emotions that lift what was previously unsubstantiated speculation to well-accepted fact.

3. *A research basis.* All the information presented in this book is drawn from systematic psychological studies that have been published in scientific journals. My research program in Japan has spanned a wide range of topics on emotion, with in-depth assessments of literally hundreds of individual Japanese living in various areas of Japan. My intent, however, is not to produce a technical report, but rather to present sound information on Japanese emotions in a form accessible to laypersons and scholars alike.

4. *An integrated theoretical framework.* Many studies of Japanese culture hold to a single point of view—sociological, anthropological, or to a lesser extent psychological. The latter part of this book integrates these three points of view in a theoretical framework for understanding Japanese culture. I believe that an integrated framework is absolutely necessary in order for cross-cultural understanding of any culture to advance.

5. *Timely relevance.* Much of the research that forms the basis of this book was conducted in the 1980s. The book is, I believe, the most current, up-to-date version of knowledge concerning emotions in Japanese culture available today.

In spite of the academic background of the research basis and integrated theoretical framework of the material presented here, the subject itself is, I believe, of great interest to laypersons as well as researchers, and to Japanese and non-Japanese alike. By focusing on emotion, I hope to offer readers a realistic and personal basis by which the Japanese people can be understood, one that has meaning for all people, regardless of culture, society, race, or country. I hope also that all readers will gain a better appreciation of the methods of inquiry that are necessary to lift anecdote and impression concerning a major aspect of life into fact. The results of high-level, scientific research need to be made more accessible to the general public, and this book is a step in that direction.

I further hope that this book accomplishes yet another goal—to complement an already impressive literature on Japanese culture and society by focusing on the feelings and emotions of the Japanese as people. It is in the trials and tribulations of being Japanese that one begins to understand the true nature of the culture, and people.

Unmasking Japan

Chapter 1

Introduction

In psychology, emotion is a well-accepted area of study, and its importance in human functioning and understanding behavior is without question. Historically, emotion has been a major component of four of the most influential scholars in the field of psychology— Freud, Piaget, Darwin, and James. Freud considered the emotion of anxiety central to his theories of the unconscious mind, defense mechanisms, and psychoanalysis. Although most psychologists know Piaget best for his work on cognitive development in children, Piaget himself identified affect (emotion) as the fuel that enables development in thinking to occur. In developing his theory of evolution, Darwin wrote about emotional expressions as one of the best-known aspects of behavior that was evolutionarily adaptive and generalizable across species. James, known to many as one of the founders of American psychology, found emotions to be as important to the understanding of human behavior as motivation (the will) and consciousness.

Emotion has become central to many studies in psychology. In the field of developmental psychology, for example, researchers have examined the way in which emotions and their expression develop in children across time and generations. Social psychologists have examined the importance of emotion in social interactions, and how our emotions are influenced by the presence or absence of others.

Studies in clinical and abnormal psychology have focused on the pathology of emotion, examining the role of emotion in different psychopathologies and treatment modalities.

Indeed, emotion is a central and important topic to our understanding of human behavior. Emotions are universal; they are associated with specific behaviors; they serve as important motivators for future behavior; and they have important social meaning as what one may call cultural glue. Emotions are in many respects the most revealing indicators of cultural similarities, and of cultural differences. Everyone, regardless of race, ethnicity, or culture, has emotions. We all know about anger, disgust, or fear; we all have experienced joy and sadness. When we speak of emotions, we refer to a universal area of perception and expression that transgresses all other boundaries that divide people. Because emotions are pancultural, they provide us with the ability to understand others on a common ground.

The Universality of Emotion

The universality of emotion grounds us in our understanding. Though we may have a good understanding of the mechanics of a culture in terms of its emphases and effects, we cannot be content with purely analytic approaches to dealing with other cultures. We must also gain some idea of what people actually think and feel. Emotions provide us with a means. Only after we have arrived at some idea of what Japanese people actually feel and how they express their feelings emotionally will we have some idea of the impact of Japanese culture on the Japanese people.

Except for emotions, there are very few means of expression that allow us to understand others on a basic, human level. Numbers are universal, but because they are purely analytic tools they do not give us much insight into the psychology of another culture. (This is not necessarily true of the manipulation of numbers in mathematics, which can provide us with great insights to culture: see Stevenson, Lee, & Stigler, 1986a, b.) The existence of language is universal, but every culture speaks a different language, forcing us to learn different languages for every culture we wish to understand.

Emotions, unlike languages, are not culture-specific. Different cultures certainly have their own emotional concepts, but research has shown that a core set of emotions is common to every culture. Without knowing the language of a culture, we can still understand the expression of certain basic emotions, because emotions do not vary as languages do. It is true, however, that different cultures exert different influences on the emotions. Exactly how the culture of Japan modifies or influences emotion is the topic of this book.

EMOTION AS EXPRESSION

Emotions are associated with a variety of specific expressive behaviors. These include spoken expressions (e.g., "I am happy" or "I am sad") as well as a host of unspoken expressions that are in many situations more important in the communication process than what is actually said. Particularly in the Japanese culture, nonverbal behavior appears to be much more significant than the spoken word.

One of the primary channels of nonverbal expressions of emotion is facial expressions. Research has shown that the core emotions that are universal are expressed in exactly the same ways via facial expressions, regardless of one's culture or race. If we can gain some appreciation for the existence of these behaviors and their universality, they will give us a much more powerful tool that we can use to understand others. Another major advantage to the examination of emotional behavior is that much of enculturation in infant and childhood development is focused on the socialization of emotional behavior. Emotional expressions are often targets of the socialization process; parents, for example, will often tell their children that they should not feel or look a certain way. Children must learn, from a very early age, what kinds of expressions are appropriate for what kinds of situations.

Although a number of writers have suggested that the nonverbal behavior of Japanese people is very different from that of non-Japanese, so far there has not been any systematic report of a comprehensive line of research on this topic. Yet differences in nonverbal expressions are perhaps one of the main reasons for the problems that often occur in intercultural communication between Japanese and non-Japanese. Obviously, it makes sense to examine this aspect of Japanese behavior in detail. Emotional behavior, via facial expressions, provides us with the opportunity to understand this aspect of the Japanese in greater detail than has been done before.

EMOTION AS MOTIVATION

Emotions summarize our experiences with the world. If one experiences fear, for example, that experience of fear probably to some extent at least reflects how one is interpreting the world. Being on a roller coaster, or in a dark alley with a stranger, would probably elicit fear, and the feeling of fear would be an accurate reflection of one's summary evaluation of the situation. Emotion is in that sense a read-out device that reflects our appraisal and evaluation of the world around us.

Emotion is closely related to another important topic in psychology—motivation. Sharing the same linguistic stems, emotion and motivation are often inseparable as theoretical and conceptual constructs, and it is difficult to consider one without the other. In psychology textbooks and courses across the United States, these topics are often covered simultaneously, because of their conceptual, semantic, and practical overlap. To many theorists (e.g., Tomkins, 1962, 1963), emotion is motivation. In order to understand motivation, why people do what they do, it is imperative to understand their emotions.

Like all cultures, much of Japanese culture is designed to manage emotions. This is accomplished by the various rules and norms that individual Japanese must live by. Many of these rules concern emotion and its expression. Although superficially the existence of these rules may lead some to suspect that the Japanese are relatively emotionless people, in fact, they are highly emotional people, and to discount the importance of emotion to them would be a travesty (one that, unfortunately, has occurred all too often). This importance of emotions is reflected in the mere existence of the degree to which rules and norms regarding emotion are established and maintained in Japan. Only when we understand the effects of culture on individual emotions, and the pain that sometimes accompanies these effects, can we begin to understand truly, and appreciate deeply, the Japanese culture and people.

EMOTION AS CULTURAL GLUE

A final reason why it is important and useful to understand emotions in the Japanese culture concerns the role emotions play in the maintenance of the culture. For example, the sharing of emotions does much to unify bonds within groups. As a group of people share in work, tasks, and responsibilities, they can each experience the same emotions. The sharing of emotions serves as a kind of invisible glue that binds the group together and keeps social bonds well cemented (cf. Kemper, 1978).

But emotions can also threaten bonds. If members of a group experience dissimilar emotions, or experience emotions that are harmful to others in the group, the group can begin to fall apart. The threat of some emotions like shame also serves to maintain the culture. Shame is an emotion that acts like a social sanction. Shame in the Japanese culture is used in ways that are similar to the use of law and punishment in Western cultures, which revolve around the emotion of guilt. In Japan, the threat of shame, and actual shame when cultural rules are indeed broken, maintains social order and conformity. Emotions thus serve important functions in preserving the Japanese culture. The same is true to a certain degree for any culture, but in Japan, because of the emphasis on groups and status, emotions have special meanings, roles, and functions.

Cross-Cultural Research on Emotion

Sociologists and anthropologists alike have long recognized the importance of emotion to the understanding of societies and cultures, and many have focused on emotion in their work. Emotion is a topic of great importance to scholars across the world, and psychological societies in Europe and in Asia are increasingly witness to research groups and new societies forming around this central topic. Emotions give our lives meaning. They color events, and help us to interpret our relationship with other people and the world around us. They help to bond people of a group together, or to drive them apart. Joy, sorrow, anger, and fear are all important aspects of our lives. In fact, it is difficult to think of life and consciousness void of feeling or emotion. The study of emotion across the boundaries of cultures, societies, and nations helps us to understand not only our differences but also our similarities, because emotion is the common language that disregards social, cultural, and political barriers.

Cross-cultural research on emotion has been a very active area of research within the psychology of emotion, and it constitutes a major part of the literature concerning emotion and its relationship and importance to human functioning. Cross-cultural research, in fact, is vital to our understanding not only of emotion but of other human phenomena, and it has certain methodological advantages in that it avoids many of the variables that necessarily complicate cross-cultural studies of less universal aspects of behavior. Because of its universality, it is relatively easy to isolate emotion as a topic of study across cultures.

Cross-cultural studies on emotion and its expression have been conducted from the turn of the century, and gained much of their impetus from Darwin's ideas about emotion and expression in relation to his theory of evolution and adaptation. Because the early studies were plagued by the methodological difficulty of measuring emotion reliably and objectively, however, for nearly half a century emotion as a topic of theory and empirical work took a back seat in American psychology to work dominated by views on cognition and rational thinking.

Cross-cultural studies of emotion originally published in the 1960s and 1970s were instrumental in identifying facial expressions as a universal vehicle for expression of emotion, and therefore as an objective tool by which emotions could be measured. The knowledge that emotions and their expressions were universal, and that they could be measured validly and reliably, served to boost our conceptual understanding of emotion as a pancultural phenomenon that transcended borders, race, ethnicity, society, and culture. That knowledge in turn led to the development of facial measurement techniques that allowed for comprehensive assessment of facial movements related to emotion. With these types of tools, researchers were now equipped to carry out thoroughgoing studies of emotion from various approaches.

Since the 1970s, we have seen a wide range of studies on emotion, now well accepted as a discipline in all areas of psychology—clinical, social, personality, physiological, etc.—throughout the world. Professional research societies centering on emotion exist, involving anthropologists, sociologists, and psychologists from many different countries. Emotion, and its counterpart, motivation and consciousness, are represented as courses in many university curricula. Studies on emotion receive major support from governmental as well as private funding agencies, and there are postdoctoral research training programs that focus exclusively on the study of emotion.

Thus, although cross-cultural research on emotion has existed for well over 100 years, the remarkable surge of formal, systematic research of the past three decades has opened up new avenues. These studies have led to new ways of understanding emotion and its importance in everyday human behavior relating to such matters as stress, health and illness, social interactions, and psychopathology and psychotherapy. Much of this recent investigation in the entire field of psychology with regard to emotion is based on the early cross-cultural work on emotion, which indeed occupies a special and significant role in the history of study and thinking in contemporary psychology.

Cross-Cultural Research on Emotion and Japan

One of the most important areas of cross-cultural research on emotion has involved Japanese culture. Because most cross-cultural researchers of emotion have been based in the United States, the cultures accessible to them have been more or less limited. Japan, as an advanced, modern, and industrial culture that is relatively amenable to research efforts and yet differs markedly from European and other such industrialized, amenable cultures, has been a logical area of interest to cross-cultural researchers who have yet to gain entrance to remote and lesser-known cultures around the world. Japan belongs to the community of advanced, industrialized nations, yet it has a very different culture from any nation in the West. Many studies that we shall review in the following chapters that were conducted in Japan have found the Japanese to be quite different from Americans and Europeans measured not only in terms of emotional perception and expression but also in terms of emotional experience and antecedents.

The substantial core of information on various aspects of human emotions in the Japanese culture, derived from cross-cultural studies published in scientific journals in psychology and anthropology, represents the best source of information documented by systematic comprehensive research programs. A great part of the research reported here has been conducted by my own laboratory since the mid-1980s, and thus represents a relatively current knowledge base about human emotions in Japan.

A number of other scholars have previously examined Japanese culture and Japanese people via human emotions. Some works, for example, focus on shame or guilt (e.g., De Vos, 1986; Pelzel, 1986). Doi's analysis of the Japanese culture's focus on the emotion of *amae* is yet another example. Ishida (1986) has focused on the emotions of love and hate in the Japanese culture. Lebra's (1976, 1986) analysis of morality in Japan is also closely related to emotion. The emphasis in this book on research findings borne from systematic cross-cultural studies is not in any way intended to discount or qualify previous works based on personal observation or anecdote. Rather, these findings are meant to add to the already existing literature on Japanese culture and the Japanese people, regardless of the methods by which the previous information was obtained. Indeed, many of the ideas and observations offered by previous writers have formed the basis for much of the thinking and conceptual understanding of much of the research reported in this book, and in the scientific journals.

Other works, though they do not focus exclusively on emotion, are indirectly related to emotion in that they provide the cultural and sociological framework within which emotions are felt, expressed, and perceived in Japan. Many previous attempts have focused on analyses of Japan through macrolevel analyses of the culture of society as a whole, involving such distinctions as the individual vs. the group (e.g., Benedict, 1946), vertical vs. horizontal societies (e.g., Nakane, 1970), shame vs. guilt cultures (Benedict, 1946; Sakuta, 1967), and double standards to characterize the Japanese culture.

INDIVIDUALS VS. GROUPS

Every culture must come to grips with the tension between unique individuality and interdependence on groups (see Markus & Kitayama, 1991; Triandis, Bontempo, Villareal, Asai, & Lucca, 1988), and the Japanese are no different. Many writers have long recognized that in many ways, both obvious and subtle, the Japanese are encouraged to think first of the group (e.g., Hamaguchi & Kumon, 1982; Moeran, 1986). The Japanese culture fosters the sacrifice of individual wishes, desires, and needs for the sake of group or collective ones. Individual identity is subsumed under group identity—whether family, friends, club, company, corporation, or nation. A Japanese person is never fully independent; being Japanese means that one must always be conscious of others.

Group consciousness pervades every aspect of the Japanese life. When you meet someone for the first time in Japan, you do not meet an individual; you meet a member of a certain group. The exchange of business cards, for example, defines clearly your group membership (and status, another important dimension) to the person you meet. Telephone manners dictate that you identify yourself by the company or organization you represent. The use of language and self-address (e.g., "we Japanese . . .") is group-centered, which tends to annoy non-Japanese who are unaccustomed to such group-centered thinking. The Japanese believe that personal statements (e.g., "I believe that . . .") are rude and vulgar, even though they may simply be the way language is used in non–group oriented cultures. This group vs. individualistic orientation of the Japanese has been commented on by many previous scholars, and is a common dimension by which the Japanese culture has been analyzed and explained.

VERTICAL VS. HORIZONTAL SOCIETIES

Japan has long been called a "vertical" society—that is, a society that pays particular attention to, and maintains status differences among interactants (e.g., Nakane, 1970). One's status or role (teacher vs. student, boss vs. worker, parent vs. child, etc.) is extremely important in Japan, and many social rules exist to maintain or preserve status differences. Horizontal societies, among them the United States, tend to minimize status differences among interactants. In the United States, the tendency is to treat everyone as equals, regardless of actual or perceived status differences.

Differences between vertical and horizontal societies are apparent in several aspects of conduct, such as the use of terms of address (e.g., see Suzuki, 1973, 1986). In horizontal societies such as the United States, "I" and "you" are used to refer to oneself and another, regardless of who the "you" is in relation to the "I." In Japan, how one addresses another is entirely determined by the status relationship between the two interactants. A student, for example, would never call a teacher by his or her first name, and workers never call their bosses by their names. In Japan, persons who are of higher status than oneself are usually addressed by their status or role (e.g., *sensei*, teacher; *kacho*, section chief). This is very unlike current patterns in the United States, where it is not uncommon for students to call teachers by their first names, and for workers to call their bosses by their first names.

SHAME VS. GUILT CULTURE

It used to be quite fashionable in anthropological and sociological literature to characterize cultures according to whether they were shame or guilt cultures (Piers & Singer, 1953). The classification of a culture depended upon which emotion, shame or guilt, was used as the primary social sanction by which sociocultural order was maintained. Japan, to no one's surprise, was often characterized as a shame culture, because of the Japanese people's high degree of consciousness of others (e.g., De Vos, 1986; Pelzel, 1986). Japanese people worry about what others will think—to a degree that can at times be oppressive, since it is not only the neighbors who must be considered but also one's family, friends, workers, and just about everyone else conceivable whom one may come in contact with. All too often, the individual Japanese may feel that it is impossible to do anything for fear of its impact, actual or perceived, on someone else.

Transgression of the social order in Japan means that one must deal with the judgment of all others. The sense of having wronged means losing face in relation to others. Shame, or more precisely the threat of shame, therefore becomes the primary social sanction. This is in contrast to guilt cultures, which use individual guilt as a primary means of maintaining social order. In guilt cultures, one is expected to answer to oneself, whereas in shame cultures one is expected to answer to others.

DOUBLE STANDARDS

Non-Japanese often complain that the Japanese appear to act according to double standards. That is, they say one thing but really mean something else. The Japanese language contains expressions for a number of concepts that describe what is occurring, including *omote* vs. *ura* (front vs. back), and *tatemae* vs. *honne* (outside frame vs. true feelings). These expressions denote the fact that the Japanese have learned to say or do whatever may be socially appropriate, according to the social context, even though they may not think or feel that way. Thus, there often are hidden meanings behind what Japanese people say or feel. This occurs mainly because the Japanese have learned to express only those things that maintain harmonious relationships with others. They have institutionalized politeness, ensuring that they will say whatever is appropriate at the time (*omote, tatemae*), even though their true feelings are quite different (*ura, honne*).

This manner of giving the appearance of politeness creates enormous problems for people who are not used to dealing with such communication patterns and at the same time are almost entirely dependent on spoken words for interactional understanding. It is not uncommon for non-Japanese people to judge Japanese as insincere or untrustworthy, which is ironic because the Japanese extremely value such characteristics as sincerity and trust. One need only recognize the existence of these curiosities of the Japanese culture to realize how complex Japanese communication patterns are. What occurs on the surface is only a small part of what is being expressed. What seem like ambiguities at face value to non-Japanese are really not ambiguous to the Japanese because they place less importance and emphasis on the spoken word, and learn to judge others more by their actions over the long run.

Psychological Approaches to the Study of Emotion

Before we turn to a full account of the numerous studies conducted on emotion in Japan, it is important to review briefly here how psychological research is conducted. This introduction will allow readers who are not familiar with this type of research to understand the basic framework and mechanics under which such research is generally conducted. Psychological research differs from anthropological or sociological analyses, which have been the approach of many previous works on Japanese culture and society. This introduction will also explain the limitations of this type of research approach. Like all research approaches, findings generated from studies in psychology are bound by the methodology used to produce those findings, and the values and beliefs of the researchers who framed the question and interpreted the data. This is no less true for the research to be presented in this book, much of which is my own, and it is important for readers to understand those limitations, just as I recognize them in our own work.

MEASUREMENT

One of the most important aspects of psychological research, especially research related to emotion, is that of measurement and operationalization. In order to study emotion, we must have reliable and valid ways of measuring it. A particular type of measurement technique must produce consistent results, and it must also be valid in the sense that it actually measures what it is supposed to measure. Many studies use facial expressions of emotion as indices of expression. The technique of decomposing the facial muscle components involved in an expression into its most elemental units is grounded in the anatomy of the face, and the expressions that we search for are the same expressions that years of research have shown to be panculturally expressive of those emotions. It is with these types of criteria that we can be assured of reliability and validity in measurement.

To study judgments of emotion, or subjective experience of emotion, we use rating scales and self-report techniques. To assure consistency of data, we identify the rating scales to be used, provide ranges on the scales (for example, 0–10 points), and provide anchoring labels on the endpoints. By applying the same structural format to all respondents within a study, we can continue with a comparison of data across individuals and groups. However, because the structure of the ratings may not match the type of response the subject might have given had he or she had a choice of response format, results may in many cases be biased in one direction or another.

SAMPLING

The standard sampling technique for comparing Japanese vs. non-Japanese emotion involves the selection of a relatively small group of participants in the Japanese culture (e.g., 50–100 participants), and corresponding groups of participants in cultures to be contrasted (e.g., U.S.). Often the groups are selected from classes or university research subject pools available to the researchers. This procedure is very different from the ethnographic approaches of many anthropological studies, or the survey approach of many sociological studies, and it has certain limitations. Surveying 50–100 respondents on an emotion-related questionnaire many not result in the richness and depth of data that one may see in case studies or small sample biohistories. Yet, within the limitations of the perhaps narrow range of the pool so far as socioeconomic class is concerned, the procedure does allow an examination of the variable of interest (i.e., emotion) across a wide range of people, and in combination with statistical techniques makes it possible to draw certain conclusions. Although there is an assumption in the psychological approach concerning the samples—that is, that they are adequate representatives of their cultures—inferential statistical procedures conducted on the data allow valid generalizations.

DATA ANALYSIS AND INTERPRETATION

Because data on emotion are measured on objective, numerical bases, they are amenable to statistical analysis. Statistics are used in psychological research as tools to distill the original raw data from all the subjects into a smaller, more finite set of indices that inform us about the data set as a whole. Statistics are also used as guidelines to make decisions about the data—underlying tendencies, differences between groups, similarities within groups, and so on. Researchers can choose among many different types of statistical techniques, according to the nature of the question being addressed by the analysis and the nature of the variables that were measured and are included in the analysis. Findings reported in the scientific journals have usually been checked in the review process for the adequacy of the choice of statistics used to analyze any set of data. In cross-cultural comparisons, which constitute the bulk of research presented in this book, statistics usually involve the direct comparison of data between Japanese and non-Japanese samples. Inferences regarding the generalizability of the differences observed in the comparison are based on probability, and the field of psychology adopts a relatively conservative degree of 5 percent chance of being wrong when differences are observed.

Also, it is important to note that most findings that are thought to be reliable are not based on the results of a single study. That is, similar studies are conducted across time on the same topic, and if the same finding is generated across two or more studies, the finding is said to be replicated. Replication is an important aspect of knowledge generation in psychological research, and assures researchers that knowledge in the literature is not based on too many flukes. The conservative 5 percent margin of error when inferring differences in a single study becomes considerably smaller when findings are replicated.

RESEARCHER INFLUENCES

It is generally thought that, because psychological research deals with numbers distilled from objective measurement techniques, it is more "pure" than other social science research approaches, and freer from researcher bias. I cannot comment on the comparison across disciplines, but I can say without equivocation that psychological research is influenced heavily by researchers and their biases. These biases exist for several reasons. First, researchers choose which aspect of emotion to study, and how to study it. As mentioned above, the participants in the studies may or may not be influenced by these choices, and the types of response alternatives they have available to them when providing data. Second, researchers choose how to analyze data and interpret their findings. The choice of analytic technique may result in different findings, as will different types of transformations of the data. In addition, researchers need to make decisions concerning what the differences, and similarities, mean when they are observed. Third, samples involved in psychological research are often involved in the research because of researcher convenience. In Japan, as in the United States, most samples in psychological research are drawn from the universities in which the researchers work—in Japan, usually from the researchers' own classes.

The inherent biases and influences, common to many avenues of science, do not necessarily negate the findings, but they must be taken into consideration as the framework within which the findings should be interpreted. The most sound studies are those that recognize the existence of such biases and take steps to offset them, rather than proceed in ignorance.

Overview and Goals

Although much of the research on which this book is based is my own, I also draw on many other studies from different laboratories.

Many of the studies reported in this book are direct comparisons of Japanese v. non-Japanese data; others include general cross-cultural comparisons that included Japanese samples among many others. Regardless, I have distilled the relevant information with regard to emotions in Japan from these studies.

The next chapter discusses some of the early research on the universality of facial expressions of emotion, and its implications to understanding the basis of emotional expression in the Japanese. Chapter 3 discusses how these universal emotions are modified by culturally prescribed rules that are dictated by social circumstance. The dual existence of pancultural universality of expression and culturally prescribed rules that dictate modification of those expressions provides a platform with which many seeming contradictions about Japanese emotional behavior can be explained and understood.

Chapters 4 and 5 present findings from research that examines the subjective experience of emotion in Japan. Much of this research comes from much larger scale studies involving many different countries and thousands of participants. In these chapters, I discuss the existence of culturally dictated rules of feeling, which should give some insight into how the subjective experience of emotion in Japan can be similar to, and different from, that in Western cultures. Chapter 6 presents findings from studies on the perception of emotion, showing cultural similarities and differences in judgments and attributions of emotion. These similarities and differences serve as the basis for the intercultural misunderstandings in social interactions.

Chapter 7 examines the lexicon of emotion in Japan, and contrasts it with emotion-related language in other cultures. These types of differences are also important to recognize, because American psychologists have been quick to assume that what we mean by the word and concept of emotion is the same in all different cultures. Chapter 8 discusses some ways of understanding Japanese culture using meaningful dimensions of psychological variability. These same dimensions can be used to understand similarities and differences across a wide range of cultures, and thus are advantageous in placing our work in Japan in broad perspective. These dimensions can also be used to make a number of predictions about emotions in Japan, many of which have already been supported by the existing research, but many of which also serve as the basis for new studies in the future. The concluding chapter discusses some areas of study that I believe are particularly relevant based on the information and knowledge generated about Japanese culture and emotion to date.

Knowledge is, and should be, a forever fluid and dynamic entity. My hope is that the information on Japanese emotions presented in this book complements previous literature, and sheds new light on the specific topic of emotions in Japan. It is also my hope that this information leads to more research on this important topic in Japan, and other cultures, and that our theoretical and conceptual understanding of the culture, society, and people of Japan will be improved in some way by this information. Finally, I hope that the information provided here can be useful to those who are involved in training and applied aspects of intercultural interaction and communication, so that there can be a healthy bridge between science, theory, and application.

Chapter 2

The Face of Emotion in Japan, I

*The Universality of Facial Expressions
of Emotion*

Understanding emotions in any culture must include an analysis of facial expressions. As the seat of emotion (Tomkins, 1962, 1963), facial expressions play an important role in communicating emotions during social interactions, and they have been the subject of intensive research across and within cultures. The role of facial expressions during emotional episodes and social interactions has been well discussed by a number of researchers (e.g., Ekman, Friesen, & Ellsworth, 1972; Izard, 1971). Although much of what I present here summarizes the main points of this literature, especially concerning the importance of understanding facial expressions to gain a deeper appreciation of emotion, this chapter will elaborate particular points as they relate to the Japanese culture, both from the research angle and from what they imply about social interaction.

The face embodies perhaps one of the most complex muscle systems in the human body. The facial musculature contains over 40 visibly identifiable, functionally anatomic units. Each muscle can innervate to different intensity levels; be symmetrical or asymmetrical on either side of the face; and can onset, apex, and offset according to its own timing sequence, producing literally thousands of different types of facial expressions or configurations. The face is one of the most complex message signal sources in interpersonal communication.

Of course, one of the messages the face can communicate is emotion. People will laugh and smile when they are happy, weep when they are sad, and frown when they are angry. These emotions, and others, may be expressed slightly, with only part of the face signaling the emotions, or they may be expressed more intensely, with the full face displaying the emotion. Emotions can be blended together in the face, showing anger and fear simultaneously, or sadness with a qualifying smile. Or, facial expressions of emotion can occur in rapid succession to each other. Emotions are also hidden and concealed in the face. The face is thus a rich source of information about emotions.

The face may even be more than an output source for the display of internal emotion. Some theorists believe that facial expressions contribute to the construction of one's own emotional experience. This hypothesis, called the *facial feedback hypothesis*, was originally postulated by Darwin (1872) and later by Tomkins (1962, 1963) and Izard (1971). It states that one's own subjective feelings of emotion are dependent upon the peripheral neural feedback from the face after the emotion is expressed. The findings from a number of studies have provided some support for this hypothesis (see reviews by Laird, 1984; Matsumoto, 1987; and Winton, 1986).

To be sure, the display of emotion is not the only function of the face. The face is also engaged in many other nonemotion behaviors (Ekman & Friesen, 1969). For example, facial expressions are important regulators of speech and conversation, letting partners know when it is appropriate to speak, or that one is keyed into the conversation. Facial behaviors are also important illustrators of speech, accenting the content of spoken words. The face can also display emblematic information, carrying its own conversational messages (e.g., greeting others with the raising of one's eyebrows, winking, etc.).

In short, the face can display emotions, contribute to emotional experience, regulate conversations, illustrate speech, and provide emblematic information. It is no wonder, then, that the face commands so much attention during social interaction. Much of this attention is automatic and part of our direct conscious experience, because we have learned in socialization and enculturation to process such information efficiently and according to certain rules. Different cultures recognize the power of the face and produce many rules to regulate not only what kinds of facial behaviors are permitted in social interaction but also how appropriate it may be even to attend to the faces of others during interaction. Because the face is a rich and complex source of information, facial expressions are a natural arena of comparative study across cultures. The data that are obtained from such studies are directly relevant to the individual lives within the cultures.

The Face in Japanese Society

The Japanese, implicitly and explicitly, recognize the importance of the face perhaps better than people of any culture. To the Japanese, the face is not only a center of personal expression of individual inner states; it is also a meaningful and powerful symbol of society and culture. The face in Japanese society plays an extremely important role as the point of connection between the outer mores of the culture and the private, inner world of the individual. Japanese culture shares a close, symbiotic relationship with the face and individual psychology to produce a unique interaction between individual emotion, social norms, and culture.

In Japan perhaps more than elsewhere, facial expressions are particularly meaningful to both individuals and society, and the face receives much attention as a target of socialization. The face, and its symbols, are revered, and transgression of its symbolic meanings and the inappropriate use of facial expressions lead to social sanction and disharmony. The concern with one's "face" is not an exaggeration or preoccupation, as typically seen by many non-Japanese; it is, rather, an integral part of basic Japanese behavior aimed at managing interdependence and maintaining harmonious relationships (De Vos, 1986; Lanham, 1986).

THE FACE AS SYMBOL

As a symbol, the face in Japanese culture is comparable to what Westerners may call "image" or "reputation," and can be understood via the Japanese culture's emphasis on collective values. Because the Japanese emphasize groups and interpersonal relationships among members within groups, how one treats others and is treated by others is extremely important. This cultural tradition reinforces certain values, beliefs, and attitudes in the Japanese culture, such as its emphasis on harmony, cohesion, cooperation, obligation, obedience, and the like. These values, in turn, encourage certain kinds of individual and group-level behaviors that depend on these values and, in turn, reinforce them. Moreover, it is not only necessary to maintain interpersonal harmony; more importantly, one must be perceived as maintaining interpersonal harmony.

The Japanese concept of face embodies this concern of how one is viewed by others. One is constantly having to "maintain" one's face to other group members—that is, to keep up or maintain harmonious relationships. If one commits a social transgression by offending others or by otherwise upsetting interpersonal harmony, one runs the danger of "losing" face. Shame, as a social sanction, can occur as the result of having lost one's face to others. When one has lost face, it is too shameful or embarrassing to meet or interact with others whom one has offended through one's behavior. That is, it becomes difficult to meet face to face (*awaseru kao ga nai*). The only thing one can do in these situations is attempt to remedy the situation somehow, in order to "save" face. If one cannot save face, then one must endure the even more difficult social sanction of isolation, if necessary self-imposed.

To have offended the group and not saved face in Japan has severe ramifications. Not only does one have to suffer social punishment individually, but others—family, friends, and other associates—are also often punished, through social sanctioning or shame. This phenomenon occurs because of the interdependent nature of human relationships in Japan. Historically, the ultimate way to save face, and thus one's family and friends, was to commit suicide. Suicide provided a means by which one could atone for one's transgressions, and ensure that one's family and friends did not suffer needlessly for one's mistakes. For these reasons, suicide in Japan took on a different meaning from what it has in Western countries.

The face also symbolizes social obligations, one of the most common of which is to "show" face (*kao o dasu*). This refers to one's appearance at various events or functions, as dictated by one's position or obligations. For example, if one's client or business associate is having a party and one is invited, then one must "show" face by attending in order to not offend the host. If one failed to show face, then one would be in danger of losing face. The face also symbolizes position. For example, the Japanese refer to people who have many useful connections as people who have a broad face (*kao ga hiroi*), and it is not uncommon for Japanese who are seeking an introduction to ask if they can borrow one's face (*kao o kasshite kudasai*), much as an American might ask, "May I use your name?"

Thus, the face has many meanings that reflect basic and important aspects of the rules that Japanese culture creates for the Japanese people and the social sanctions that exist if the rules are not adhered to. Emotions are powerful and important components to human life in any culture, but in Japan the personal and symbolic meanings of the face make them especially important. The social baseline for many of these symbols, of course, lies in the actual facial expressions of the Japanese.

Are the Japanese Different in Their Facial Expressions of Emotion?

Scholars and laypersons alike have long held the belief that the Japanese were entirely different from Westerners in their facial displays of emotion. Japanese literature, from the Fujiwara period's *Genji Monogatari* through Tanizaki, Kawabata, and Mishima of more recent history, is replete with examples of how personal emotional behavior of the Japanese is inseparable from Japanese society and culture, being different or "foreign" to Western cultures. More formal studies in cultural and psychological anthropology, from Benedict's *Chrysanthemum and the Sword* (1946) to the work of Lebra (1976) and De Vos (1973), also point clearly to the ways in which Japanese modes of expression differ from those of Westerners. Invariably, these works highlight the extremes of the Japanese emotional repertoire, from their "inscrutability" to their displays of outlandish exaggerated emotion. Altogether, we have inherited a dual stereotype of the Japanese as either emotionless robots or extravagantly emotional actors.

In fact, the formal study of cultural differences in emotional expression has its roots in theoretical works that postulated exactly the opposite, that people of different cultures expressed emotions in exactly the same ways (i.e., cultural universality). The first and most often cited author who held this view was Darwin, who, while conducting the research for his theory of evolution, noted the seemingly amazing similarities in emotional expressions between humans and nonhuman primates. Darwin (1872) suggested that emotions were biologically innate, evolutionarily adaptive, and displayed in exactly the same ways across human and nonhuman primates, and across cultures within humans. His chapter on emotion, however, originally intended for *On the Origin of Species*, was so long that it was published as a separate monograph entitled *The Expression of Emotion in Man and Animals*. In it, Darwin included many illustrations of human and nonhuman primate emotional expressions drawn in painstaking detail to portray the similarities in emotional expression across species. Unfortunately, *On the Origin of Species* drew so much attention that the monograph on emotions was largely neglected (Ekman, 1973).

After Darwin, the view that emotions were universal received only occasional support. Allport (1924), Asch (1952), and Tomkins (1962, 1963) all argued for cultural invariants in facial behaviors related to emotion, though from different theoretical standpoints. But lacking direct evidence to support their claims, their work, too, received scant notice.

Meanwhile, the notion that emotional expressions were culture-specific, learned like a language, and different for each culture, grew in strength. The writings of LaBarre (1947, 1962) and Birdwhistell (1970), which postulated cultural differences in emotional behavior, received wide attention and were generally accepted as evidence that facial behavior associated with emotion was socially learned and culturally variable. Although these writers, too, lacked quantitative evidence, relying instead on anecdotal impressions, descriptions of novelists, and anthropological reports, the culture-specific view of emotional expressions became the more prevalent view over time. This view accorded well with early accounts of Japanese cultural differences in expressivity. Western scholars such as Ruth Benedict and Margaret Mead found it difficult to understand the cultural differences in emotional expressions of the Japanese. Early anthropological works on Japan and Japanese culture helped to solidify the view that emotional expressions were culture-specific.

Before 1960, only four studies attempted to address the universality or culture-specificity issue. These studies (Dickey & Knower, 1941; Triandis & Lambert, 1958; Vinacke, 1949; Vinacke & Fong, 1955) reported either cultural similarities or differences in emotional expression, but the validity of their findings was handicapped by methodological flaws, including the validity of the stimuli they used to portray emotion, the generalization of their stimulus persons, and the degree of mutual contact among the cultural groups tested (Ekman, 1973).

Thus, without evidence to support the universal view of facial expressions of emotion, the consensus grew that facial expressions were culture-specific, learned like a language, and different for different cultures. Following Benedict and Mead, who concluded that the Japanese express emotions differently from people of other cultures such as the American, French, and German, other scholars in anthropology and psychology, as well as laypersons, adopted this view as a plausible explanation of the seemingly large cultural differences in the emotional behaviors of the Japanese. It was not until the late 1960s and early 1970s that research produced clear, unambiguous evidence for the existence of universal facial expressions of emotion, including the expressions of the Japanese.

Evidence for the Universality of Facial Expressions of Emotion

The earliest systematic evidence for the universality of facial expressions of emotion came from several different types of studies, conducted in most part by Paul Ekman and Wallace Friesen at the University of California, San Francisco, in collaboration with Sylvan Tomkins, who had just published a theoretical treatise on emotion postulating cultural invariants in facial displays of emotion (Tomkins, 1962, 1963). Tomkins persuaded Ekman and Friesen, and independently Carroll Izard, to test his ideas concerning universality.

Some of the earliest evidence for cultural universals came from a series of judgment studies conducted by Ekman and Friesen, and Izard. In one of their better known studies, Ekman and Friesen (1971) took photographs depicting various facial expressions of emotion to five countries: the United States, Japan, Chile, Argentina, and Brazil. The photographs used in this study were specially selected by Ekman, Friesen, and Tomkins and were considered examples of universal emotions. The researchers asked members in each of these countries to name the emotion they thought was being expressed in the face. If emotions are universal, all the people would judge the expressions as exactly the same emotion, regardless of their country or culture; but if emotions are culturally relative, the judgments of the expressions would differ according to which country or culture the person was from.

To their surprise, Ekman and Friesen found that six emotions were judged with consistently high agreement across all five cultures, thus supporting the universalist position. The evidence for universality meant that the Japanese interpreted the emotions in exactly the same ways as did people in the other, very different cultures. The six emotions were anger, disgust, fear, happiness, sadness, and surprise.

Izard's (1971) study, conducted independently but according to the same methodological procedures, produced exactly the same finding. His study included a second sample of Japanese observers, in addition to judges from France, Switzerland, Greece, and Africa. Thus, the evidence for universality was replicated on an independent sample of Japanese judges, confirming that the Japanese were no different from people of other cultures in attributing emotions to the facial expressions. These data provided the first type of evidence for universality in emotional expressions.

These studies came under criticism from some who suggested that a shared visual input among the cultures studied (through mass media, movies, etc.) could allow members of different cultures to learn what people of other cultures looked like when they expressed emotion. Thus, the findings for universality may have been confounded by the shared learning of the various emotions from different cultures. This criticism was especially salient because all the posers of the expressions in the photos judged were Caucasian, and observers in non-Caucasian cultures such as Japan would automatically know that the poser was not a member of their own culture. It was suggested that when judging such people, the observers might have applied rules about emotion that they learned through the mass media about what Americans look like when they are feeling emotion.

In order to address these criticisms, Ekman and Friesen took their studies to two preliterate tribal cultures in New Guinea. Since these tribes had very little contact with the Western world, shared visual input could not possibly account for cultural agreement in judgments or expressions of emotion. In two studies (Ekman & Friesen, 1971; Ekman, Sorenson, & Friesen, 1969), Ekman and Friesen replicated the results from the previous judgment studies, showing that the New Guinea tribal people interpreted the facial stimuli in exactly the same ways as did the judges in the earlier studies. These data laid to rest criticisms concerning the validity of their earlier findings. These data provided the second type of evidence for universality.

Before leaving New Guinea, Ekman and Friesen also asked the New Guineans to pose the various emotions on their faces. Unedited videotapes of these poses were shown to American observers, who were asked to judge which emotions were being portrayed. In spite of the fact that none of the Americans had seen or had any sort of contact whatsoever with New Guineans, they were able to judge which emotions were being portrayed with high accuracy (Ekman & Friesen, 1971). These data provided a third type of evidence for the pancultural universality of facial expressions of emotion.

Still, there was another loophole that needed to be looked at. All the research conducted so far had to do with judgments of emotional expressions, not the emotional expressions per se. It might have been possible that judgments were universal, but that people actually showed different emotions when emotions were aroused spontaneously. What was necessary was to examine the actual expressions people from different cultures displayed when emotions were aroused, and to demonstrate that those expressions were indeed the same.

To this end, Ekman and Friesen compared the spontaneous emotional reactions of Japanese with American subjects. In this study (Ekman, 1972; Friesen, 1972), people from both cultures were brought to a laboratory where they watched intense, stress-inducing films, including a burn scene, an amputation, childbirth with forceps, and an aboriginal puberty rite. A hidden video camera recorded their facial expressions, which were then coded by means of a facial measurement technique known as the Facial Affect Scoring Technique (FAST). FAST decomposed the expressions that occurred into their most elemental and basic anatomical units, or components. A comparison of the components displayed by the Japanese with those displayed by the Americans indicated that the Japanese exhibited exactly the same expression components of emotion as did the Americans at exactly the same points during the film. These data formed yet the fourth type of evidence for the universality of facial expressions of emotion.

Additional studies that have been conducted in the two decades since the publication of this first series of studies have in all cases replicated the earlier findings (e.g., Ekman et al., 1987; Matsumoto & Ekman, 1989; and reviews by Matsumoto, 1991, and Matsumoto, Wallbott, & Scherer, 1989). Evidence has also been found for the universality of a seventh facial expression of emotion—that of contempt (Ekman & Friesen, 1986; Ekman & Heider, 1988; Matsumoto, 1992b). This research also included samples from Japan, ensuring that the Japanese data were comparable with data obtained elsewhere.

Consequently, the universality of emotional expressions is no longer debated in academic circles; contrary to overriding popular belief concerning Japanese facial expressions, the Japanese can, and do, express the universal emotions in exactly the same ways as people of other cultures. That facial expressions of emotion are universal and biologically innate may be surprising to readers whose experiences are steeped in cultural differences. To believe that the Japanese express emotion in exactly the same ways as do Americans, French, Germans, and everyone else is contrary to almost everything Westerners have come to know about the Japanese.

These opposing points of view can be reconciled by the recognition and understanding that the existence of pancultural elements in facial expressions of emotion does not imply the absence of any cultural differences in the face and emotion. More specifically, universality in the facial components does not necessarily rule out the existence of culturally specific rules that govern their usage. Universality, in other words, suggests that cultural differences are not revealed by particular facial behaviors associated with specific emotions but rather lie in the circumstances that bring about emotions (emotion antecedents), or in the behavior that occurs as a result of emotion (emotion consequences), or in the rules governing the management of facial displays of universal emotions depending upon social circumstance (display rules). Subsequent chapters in this book discuss these topics in detail.

The Universal Facial Expressions of Emotion

Examples of the seven universal emotions can be found in any introductory psychology textbook, and in other sources (e.g., Ekman & Friesen, 1975), but the examples given here are the first presentations of Japanese renditions of the universal emotions. All the photographs come from Matsumoto and Ekman's (1988) set of photographs known as the Japanese and Caucasian Facial Expressions of Emotion (JACFEE), a set of 56 color photos of each of the seven universal emotions. There are eight examples of each emotion, four posed by Caucasians and four posed by Japanese (two males and two females each). Each poser appears only once in the entire set, eliminating power redundancy across stimuli. The expressions have been coded using Ekman and Friesen's (1978) Facial Action Coding System (FACS), which decomposes each of the expressions into its basic and most elemental functionally anatomic units. FACS coding has ensured that the expressions match exactly the universal emotions found in earlier research (see Ekman & Friesen, 1975). The JACFEE has been used in judgment studies conducted by my laboratory in the United States, Japan, India, Poland, and Hungary, and with Vietnamese refugees. The JACFEE has also been used in judgments studies by other researchers in many other countries and cultures. The expressions portrayed have consistently produced high agreement concerning the interpretation of the emotion portrayed. To our knowledge, this is the only stimulus set including posers of visibly different races that meets psychometric criteria for validly and reliably portraying the universal emotions.

A brief note is in order here concerning the significance of the availability of multiracial poses such as those in the JACFEE. Many previous judgment studies of emotion, such as those reported earlier in this chapter, used posers basically of one racial group, that of Caucasians. Observers in non-Caucasian cultures are of course quite aware that the posers are not from the observer's own culture. This methodological problem is not as problematic when universality—or agreement—in judgments across cultures is sought, because the noncongruence of the race between the poser and the observers should act to produce spurious differences, not similarities, in judgments. Noncongruence between poser and observer race is, however, a major methodological limitation when attempting to untangle cultural differences in judgments. A number of studies that have documented cultural differences in judgments of the universal emotions have required the use of multiracial stimuli in order to determine whether the differences observed were limited to judgments of others of one's own or other racial backgrounds. The JACFEE was developed for this purpose.

In brief, the JACFEE portrays facial prototypes—still-image portrayals of full-faced expressions of each of the seven emotions. The reliability of these expressions to portray universally each of the emotions is supported by data spanning at least twenty different cultures over two and a half decades of cross-cultural research. Here, I present only examples of a Japanese male and female displaying each emotion. Examples of Caucasian males and females displaying the same emotion can be found in Ekman and Friesen (1975). A comparison of the expressions of the Japanese posers presented here with the Caucasian posers presented in Ekman and Friesen (1975) will show that the expressions are exactly the same. In discussing the various facial components that make up each of the expressions, it is useful to observe appearance changes in three facial areas: the upper face, including the area above the eyes; the eyes; and the lower face, including the area under the eyes—cheeks and mouth area.

ANGER

Anger is perhaps one of the most powerful and dangerous emotions that exists. The inappropriate expression of anger can be devastating to interpersonal relationships, which is why so much of emotion socialization in Japan and elsewhere is centered around controlling anger. On the other hand, anger is one way of maintaining status differences, since anger can often be appropriate for higher-status persons to express toward lower-status others.

When anger does occur and its expression is uninhibited, anger is expressed in all three areas of the face (see Figures 1a and 1b). The eyebrows are drawn down and together, the upper eyelid is raised, giving the expression a staring quality; the lips are pushed together; and the lips are tightened. Another version of the universal expression of anger includes the same components as those presented above, with the exception that the upper eyelid is not raised; rather, the upper and lower eyelids are both tensed (see Figure 1c).

In one study, we examined how the tensing or raising of the upper eyelid in the anger expression affected, if at all, the overall message of anger (Matsumoto, 1989b). These same photos were presented to both American and Japanese observers, who were asked (1) to

Fig. 1. Japanese Expressions of Emotion

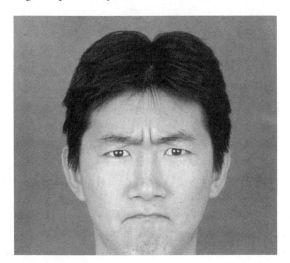

1a. Male Anger

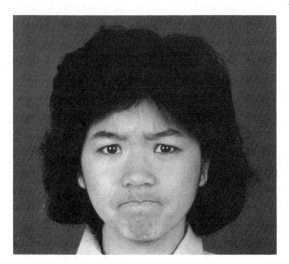

Fig. 1b. Female Anger

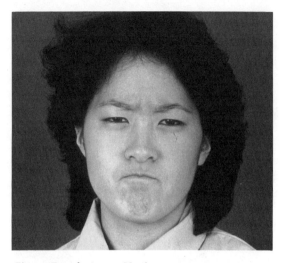

Fig. 1c. Female Anger, Version 2

judge which emotion was being portrayed, and (2) how intensely it was being expressed. Analysis of the observer's judgments of which emotion was expressed indicated no differences between the two cultures; both cultures agreed to the same degree that anger was the emotion being expressed. There were, however, some cultural differences in the degree of intensity attributed to the expressions. The Caucasian photos with the upper eyelid raised were judged more intensely than the Caucasian photos with the upper eyelid tensed, by both American and Japanese judges. The opposite was found for Japanese photos: the Japanese photos with the eyelids tensed together were judged more intensely than the Japanese photos with the upper eyelid raised. These findings suggest that facial physiognomy, that is, the overall structure of the face, may interact with the universal emotional expressions to produce cultural differences in subtle messages accompanying the emotion, although the overall emotion message may be the same.

CONTEMPT

Contempt is the latest emotion that research has shown to be universally expressed (Ekman & Friesen, 1986; Ekman & Heider, 1988;

Matsumoto, 1992b). Like anger, contempt is a potentially dangerous emotion, because its expression can be harmful to interpersonal relationships. Its full-face expression is relatively simple, and involves only the tightening of the lip corner on a single side of the face (see Figures 1a and 1e). The contempt expression can be very slight and very fast. Often you can see this expression occur immediately after someone has said something; it will flash on and off the face very quickly. In this case, the contempt may be accenting what the person is trying to say, or expressing an underlying emotional state. It is also common to see the contempt expression appear gradually on a person's face, as he or she listens to a conversation that he or she doesn't like. In these cases, the tightening of the lip corners can be very, very slight.

Because the full-face expression of anger is much more involved and complex than the full-face expression of contempt, the Japanese take extra caution not to express anger inappropriately. Although one will see less uninhibited anger in social situations, less care is taken to hide or suppress the subtle expressions such as contempt; thus, one will see expressions of contempt much more readily in Japan than one will see anger.

DISGUST

Like anger and contempt, disgust is also a negative emotion. But unlike the first two, disgust is usually a reaction to something that is repulsive. Smelling spoiled milk, for example, will bring about expressions of disgust, as would eating something rotten. The English word disgust is also used in other situations; for example, it is common for people to say that they are disgusted by someone else, or by a particular situation or circumstance. One should note, however, that the English word disgust is not easily translated into Japanese, which suggests cultural differences in the concept of this emotion (see also Chapter 7).

The key feature to the disgust expression is the wrinkling of the nose (see Figures 1f and 1g). It may appear that these posers are also tightening their eyelids, but that is not the case. Wrinkling the nose strongly will cause the appearance of the eyes to be tensed, when in fact the muscles around the eyes are not really being innervated.

Fig. 1d. Male Contempt

Fig. 1e. Female Contempt

Fig. 1f. Male Disgust

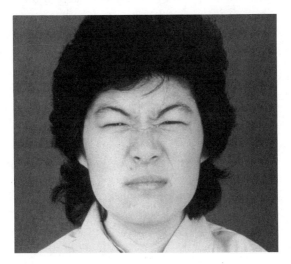

Fig. 1g. Female Disgust

FEAR

Fear is another emotion that we have all experienced. With fear, we often feel a host of other bodily symptoms, such as heart palpitations, chill, or trembling. Fear is a basic primary emotion that tells us that we may be in danger, and that we should do something about it. The expression of fear is much more complex than that of contempt or disgust. Its basic components are spread across the three facial areas: the brows are raised, and then pulled together while being raised; the upper eyelid is raised; the lower eyelid is tensed; the lips may or may not part; the lip corners are stretched sideways (see Figures 1h and ii).

This expression is very difficult to do voluntarily. This is because some of the muscle movements involved in this expression are naturally antagonistic to each other. For example, raising one's eyebrows and pulling them together while raised are antagonistic movements— not necessarily difficult to do by themselves, but very difficult to do together. When elicited spontaneously in a natural situation, however, people can produce this expression with no hesitation, despite the fact that the muscle movements are antagonistic to each other. I have witnessed this facial muscle patterning in infants many times as their fathers toss them high into the air. This speaks to the power of the innate facial blueprint system.

In the study mentioned above (Matsumoto, 1989b), we examined how the degree of upper eyelid raise affects the message of fear for Caucasian and Japanese posers. We presented American and Japanese observers with two different fear expressions posed by Caucasians and Japanese, one with a low degree of upper eyelid raise and one with a high degree of raise. Judges of both cultures rated the Caucasian male and female, and Japanese female photos of fear with the high degree of upper eyelid raise as more intense than the photos with less upper eyelid raise. The opposite was found, however, for Japanese male photos: those with less upper eyelid raise were judged more intense than those with a high degree of upper eyelid raise. These findings suggested to us again that racial differences in facial physiognomy may interact with the universal expressions of emotion and contribute to cultural differences in the overall messages sent via the face.

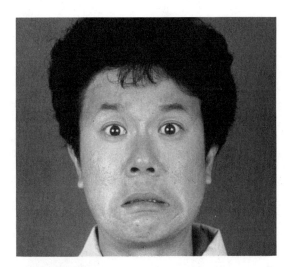

Fig. 1h. Male Fear

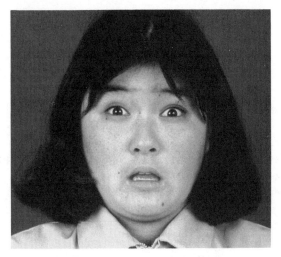

Fig. 1i. Female Fear

HAPPINESS

Happiness can play an important function as a social glue, serving to strengthen bonds among members within a group, and between groups. The expression used to display one's joy or happiness is, of course, the smile. There are two basic components to the expression of happiness: the muscles surrounding the eyes are tightened, and the lips are pulled up and to the corner. When people are asked to smile, or to think about expressions of happiness, they often forget about the muscle around the eyes and concentrate only on the smile of the lower face. But in expressions of true "joy" or "happiness," both parts of the face must be involved (see Figures 1j and 1k).

The smile is the expression most often used to conceal or mask one's emotions in situations where the expression of one's true feelings may be inappropriate. When a person smiles to conceal emotions and does not truly feel happiness or joy, the muscle around the eyes will not be tightened. In Japan, people of lower status may smile to denote acceptance of a command or order by a person of higher status when in fact they feel anger or contempt for the order or the person giving the order. Because it is inappropriate to express one's negative feelings in such a situation, it is common to conceal these emotions by smiling. Invariably, these "submission" smiles will lack the muscle surrounding the eye.

Smiles are also used to simulate or fake happiness. In interpersonal situations, the Japanese will often smile not to express true joy or to conceal negative emotions but to simulate positive emotion, to signal acceptance by understanding, or even to elicit compliance. It is not uncommon, for example, for higher-status Japanese people to smile when addressing lower-status others, even in the absence of true positive emotion.

One can test the effect of the tightening of the muscles around the eyes by looking at oneself in a mirror. Smile first as if you feel true joy or happiness: bring the corners of your lips up and make sure you tighten the muscle around your eyes. You might even laugh, and if you do, see how your eyes become really constricted. Now try to smile by only pulling the corners of your lips up without tightening the muscle around your eyes. You should notice a big difference, not only in the single absence of the eye muscle but in the overall message

Fig. 1j. Male Happiness

Fig. 1k. Female Happiness

conveyed by the expression. One is simply not happy when displaying this expression.

SADNESS

Sadness and distress are other common emotions. There are many reasons why people become sad—ranging from the loss of a loved person to vague feelings of melancholy and depression. Sadness is expressed facially in all three areas of the face: the inner corners of the eyebrows are raised and drawn together; the eyes may or may not look downward; the muscle surrounding the eyes will be tightened; the lower lip will push up; and the corners of the lips will be pulled down (see Figures 1l and 1m).

One will often see the inner corners of the eyebrows rise on their own when people are talking, without the other lower face components. This is because some facial expressions are also used as punctuators or illustrators—signals that illustrate the content of speech. The upper-face part of sadness is often used as an illustrator; when it occurs alone without the lower face of sadness, it should not be confused with the expression of sadness.

The raising of just the inner corners of the eyebrows is another difficult movement to perform voluntarily. The muscle above the eyebrows is actually a single muscle known as the frontalis muscle, but it has two functionally different movements: the inner portion of the muscle can move independently of the outer portions. Perhaps only 20–25 percent of the people I have come in contact with can raise just the inner corners of the eyebrows without raising the outer corners at the same time. You will see this expression, however, occur spontaneously and without hesitation.

SURPRISE

Surprise is the last of the seven universal facial expressions of emotion. It usually occurs in reaction to an unexpected event or situation, and is often quickly followed by another emotion, such as happiness (e.g., unexpectedly meeting an old friend), or fear (e.g., suddenly seeing a car coming toward you). At other times, surprise occurs simultaneously with other emotions, blended together.

Surprise is expressed in all three areas of the face: the brows (both inner and outer) are lifted; the upper eyelids are raised slightly; and

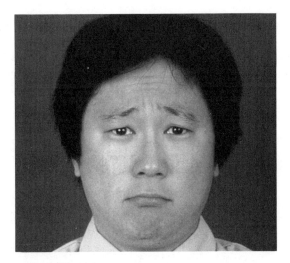

Fig. 1l. Male Sadness

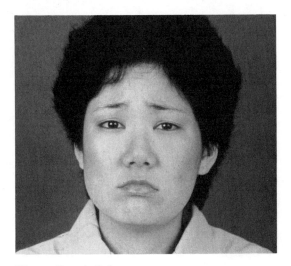

Fig. 1m. Female Sadness

Fig. 1n. Male Surprise

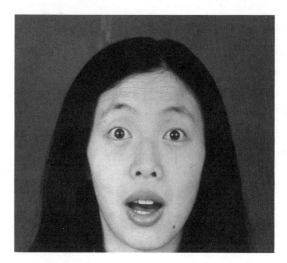

Fig. 1o. Female Surprise

the jaw is dropped (see Figures 1n and 10). The raising of the brows is a facial action that is also used as a speech illustrator, much like the raising of the inner corners of the eyebrows in sadness. The raising and lowering of the brows often coincides quite well with the pitch of one's speech. Raising the brows, for example, often occurs with a rise in pitch; lowering the brows often occurs with a lowering of pitch. When this type of facial action occurs, it is important not to confuse these movements with signs of actual surprise.

Conclusion

Cross-cultural research, including different samples of Japanese respondents across many studies and two decades of research, has proved the existence of seven facial expressions of emotion that are biologically innate and universal in that prototypes of these emotions are programmed genetically in everyone: the Japanese, when allowed, will express these seven emotions in exactly the ways shown in this chapter. One can witness these expressions in Japanese people when the situation or circumstance is such that they feel "safe" in expressing the emotions—that is, when the rules of the culture dictate that it is permissible to express them. In another situation, however, these very same people may display something entirely different even in reference to the same emotion, because the situation demands it.

If this is true, how can the Japanese facial expressions be said to be universal? We perceive many fundamental differences in the behavior of Japanese people, but we recognize that all people in all cultures learn, from infancy and childhood through adulthood, to manage the universal facial expressions of emotion to conform to cultural mores and values. People learn rules called cultural display rules that dictate how to modify emotional expressions, depending on the social situation or circumstance. These are not rules on how to create new expressions; rather, they are rules for the appropriate use of the universal emotions. In Japan, many of the display rules are derived from the Japanese cultural emphases on groups and status. It is in the world of display rules where we can come to a better understanding of how and why the Japanese often differ from westerners and others in their displays of emotion.

Chapter 3

The Face of Emotion in Japan, II

Culture-Specific Aspects and Display Rules

Proof of the existence of universal facial expressions of emotion answered some important questions concerning cultural similarities in expression, but there were still many questions remaining. For example, how is it that our everyday experiences with people of different cultures tell us that their emotional expressions are universal, even though we can readily observe people of one culture weeping openly at funerals, while people of other cultures may smile? Why do people of some cultures freely express their anger at others, while others show nothing? How is it that noted scholars like Ray Birdwhistell and Margaret Mead could have come to the conclusion that facial expressions of emotion are culture-specific, learned like a language, and different for different cultures? To answer these questions, and to reconcile the coexistence of pancultural universality and cultural specificity in emotional expressions, research had to be done on what we now know to be cultural display rules.

The Neurocultural Theory of Emotion

Early in their research program on the universality of emotion, Ekman and Friesen pondered the possible coexistence of cultural similarities and differences in facial expressions of emotion. They coined the term *display rules* to describe the rules that people learn early in life to manage or modify their facial expressions of emotion, depending on social circumstances (Ekman & Friesen, 1969). Based totally on cultural mores and social appropriateness, the notion of display rules offered researchers and theorists alike a mechanism by which cultural differences could exist in spite of, or rather in addition to, biologically innate, pancultural facial expressions of emotion.

Ekman and Friesen called their theory the neurocultural theory of emotional expression (1969; Ekman, 1972). This theory posits the existence of a biologically innate Facial Affect Program, which stores the facial prototypes of the universal emotions in the brain. As shown in the preceding chapter, there are seven universal facial expressions, which, being biologically innate, are exactly the same for all people, regardless of race, culture, or gender. When an emotion is triggered, a signal is sent to the Facial Affect Program; it, in turn, sends a message to the face to express the emotion. Before reaching the face, however, the signal from the Facial Affect Program may be influenced by signals from other parts of the brain that store the cultural display rules. These rules may or may not modify the original signal sent by the Facial Affect Program. The resulting output in terms of facial display thus represents the joint influence of both a biologically innate facial affect program (storing the facial prototypes of each of the universal emotions) and the culturally prescribed display rules (see Figure 2).

Although the information stored in the biologically innate Facial Affect Program is necessarily fixed, the information stored as cultural display rules is not. The number and extent of these rules are entirely dependent upon the culture from which the rules are produced. Cultures may have rules to: *deamplify expressions*—to show less emotion than you actually feel; *neutralize expressions*—to show nothing even though you feel something; *amplify or exaggerate expressions*—to show more than what you actually feel; *mask or conceal expressions*—to show something other than what you really feel; *blend expressions*—to mix the expressions of two or more emotions together simultaneously. These rules are learned early in life and become part of everyone's automatic repertoire of emotion.

The existence of display rules, and support for the neurocultural theory of emotional expression, was documented early on by Ekman and Friesen. In the last chapter, I described a study they conducted involving American and Japanese participants viewing intense, stress-

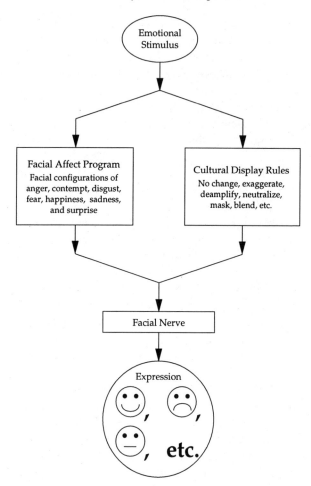

Fig. 2. Ekman and Friesen Neurocultural Theory of Emotion with Facial Affect Program and Cultural Display Rules. Adapted from P. Ekman (1972), *Universals and cultural differences in facial expressions of emotion.* In J. Cole (Ed.), *Nebraska Symposium of Motivation,* 1971 (Vol. 19). Lincoln: University of Nebraska Press.

inducing stimuli as their facial behaviors were videotaped without their knowledge (Ekman, 1972; Friesen, 1972). In one condition, the participants viewed the stimuli alone. Their facial behaviors were coded using Ekman, Friesen, and Tomkins's Facial Affect Scoring Technique (FAST). The coding indicated that both the Americans and the Japanese exhibited exactly the same facial expressions of disgust, sadness, anger, and fear. These findings provided clear support for the universality of emotional expressions.

This same study also included another condition involving the same participants. In the second part of the study, each of the participants viewed the stressful stimuli again, but this time in the presence of a higher-status experimenter. To emphasize the status differences between the participants and the researcher, the experimenter was an older male who wore clothes suitable to his status—shirt, slacks, tie, and white lab coat. The experimenter sat in front of the participants, in clear view of their facial behaviors, as they viewed the stimuli. As before, their facial behaviors were videorecorded without their awareness, and again coded with FAST. Facial coding indicated that, whereas the Americans on the whole still exhibited the same negative emotions as in the first part of the experiment, the Japanese expressions were different, not only from the Americans' but also from their own emotions in the earlier experiment. In every instance in which the Americans showed negative emotions, the Japanese either showed no emotions or smiled.

Ekman and Friesen suggested that the differences in facial displays occurred because of cultural differences in display rules. In the first part of the experiment, in which the participants viewed the stimuli apparently unobserved, the participants had no need to modify their expressions, and the Japanese showed exactly the same expressions as did the Americans. In the second part of the experiment, when the participants viewed the stimuli in the presence of a higher-status experimenter, cultural display rules came into play and the Japanese participants modified their behavior to become socially appropriate. A Japanese display rule to conceal one's negative feelings in the presence of someone of higher status forced them to mask their negative feelings with a smile. The Americans, having no such cultural display rule, exhibited essentially the same expressions as before.

The findings from this study were of considerable import because they provided researchers, theorists, and laypersons alike with a way to understand and explain the dual existence and influence of universal and culturally specific facial expressions of emotion. Display rules allow cultures, and the individual members within cultures, to control universal emotions to suit social situations or circumstances. When display rules are not of consequence, the Japanese will exhibit exactly the same facial expressions of emotion as will people of any other culture. Yet when the social situation calls for the use of display rules, the Japanese will modify their expressions in order to be socially appropriate.

Why do Display Rules Exist in Japan?

The study just described involving Japanese participants was important because it was the first to document the existence of display rules. We have now come to realize that display rules are an integral part of any culture and that they exist because groups of people must have rules governing social interaction and behavior in order to control individual behavior and permit group survival. Just as societies have laws governing overt behavior, cultures have social laws that we call display rules that govern emotional behaviors. The mere existence of these social laws or display rules speaks to the importance of emotion to individual and group-level functioning, and to the necessity of groups to monitor and moderate them.

Like all cultures, that of the Japanese has many different rules that govern social life and interaction. These rules represent the ritualized ways by which the Japanese culture has contrived in the course of its history to make the most efficient use of its human and natural resources in order to survive. The particular characteristics of Japan— its island existence, relatively high population density, the availability of land and other natural resources to feed the population—all contribute to these social laws and display rules.

In order to come to a better understanding of the importance of display rules in Japan, one must first comprehend the importance of emotion. Emotions serve several important functions in Japan. On the personal level, emotions give meaning to life, accenting events as they occur and emotions are aroused in reaction. Emotions also serve as motivators for future personal behavior, and thus help to shape, or maintain, one's behavior within a social context. Emotions also have meaning on an interpersonal level. Emotions can facilitate and develop bonds between individuals. In a collective society such as Japan's, this aspect of the emotions is very important, because emotions become the social glue that maintains group harmony and cohesion. Emotions also help to maintain differences between one's ingroups and outgroups. In Japan, differentiating between ingroups and outgroups is just as important a social function as maintaining cohesion within one's ingroup. Emotions also differentiate status differences in that they can both display deference from lower-status persons to those of higher status; and display superiority from higher to lower.

Display rules are in fact the Japanese culture's way of ensuring that the "correct" emotions serve the "appropriate" social function in maintaining the social and cultural pattern. By encouraging some emotions and discouraging others, display rules ensure that ingroups maintain harmony and cohesion, while outgroups are differentiated; they ensure that status differences among social interactants are maintained. Display rules are the Japanese culture's ways of providing individual members with guidelines so as to maintain the culture's and society's emphasis on groups and status differences. To the extent that this maintenance is important for the culture's and society's survival and functioning, display rules serve a necessary purpose.

The process of learning display rules begins early in life—perhaps, some researchers suggest, as a result of the early childrearing practices of Japanese mothers. Although the question is far from being answered completely, support for this idea has been offered by a number of researchers (Bradshaw, Miyake, Campos, Kanaya, & Usui, 1990; Camras, Campos, Oster, & Bradshaw, 1990; Oster, 1990). Certainly by early childhood (say three to four years of age) the Japanese child is well on the way to learning many of Japanese society's appropriate cultural display rules. The Japanese tolerate little individual variation in display rules and have several social penalties, if you will (shame, isolation, being outcast, etc.), to ensure that members adhere to these rules. This is not to say that individual differences do not exist, but display rules perform an important and necessary function in helping to maintain the culture's emphasis on groups and status differences.

More Recent Research on Cultural Display Rules

Following the publication of the original universality research of Ekman, Friesen, and Izard, and of the original display rule research by Ekman and Friesen, there was a temporary lull in cross-cultural research on the emotions. Ekman, Friesen, and Izard themselves turned their attentions to studying other aspects of the emotions. Ekman and Friesen, for example, spent considerable time during the mid- to late 1970s refining their facial measurement system, developing what is now known to be the most comprehensive facial coding system available, the Facial Action Coding System (FACS—Ekman & Friesen, 1978). Izard turned his research attention to studying the development of emotional expression and recognition in infants and young children. Because of their pioneering efforts, the study of emotion is now well accepted in many areas of psychology, including, clinical, developmental, personality, physiological, and of course, social psychology.

Although there were few cross-cultural studies conducted during this time period, numerous within-culture studies in the United States examined the development of display rule knowledge (see reviews by Camras, 1985; Cole, 1985; Malatesta & Haviland, 1985; Michalson & Lewis, 1985; Saarni, 1985). In general, many of these studies seem to indicate that the ages of six through ten are particularly important to the development of early display rules (though these ages may simply reflect methodological limitations in our ability to study display rules as verbal concepts, since it is much more difficult for various reasons to study such concepts in younger children. A number of studies also examined various social influences on emotional expression, such as the inhibition or exaggeration of expressions depending on the presence of others (see Blumberg, Solomon, & Perloe, 1981; Kilbride & Yarczower, 1980; Kleck, Vaughan, Cartwright-Smith, Vaughan, Colby, & Lanzetta, 1976; Kraut, 1982; Yarczower & Daruns, 1982; Yarczower, Kilbride, & Hill, 1979). These studies generally showed that social factors contribute greatly to expression facilitation or suppression.

Still, many questions about cultural similarities and differences in emotional expressions and display rules remain unanswered. Until very recently (Matsumoto, 1991), there has not been one published, cross-cultural study examining similarities or differences in display rules or spontaneous emotional expressions since the original display rules studies by Ekman (1972) and Friesen (1972), nor has our theoretical understanding of cultural display rules advanced since Ekman and Friesen's original formulation of them in 1969.

In an attempt to address this gap in our knowledge, our laboratory recently conducted the first cross-cultural follow-up study on cultural display rules (Matsumoto, 1991). In this study, we asked American and Japanese participants how appropriate it would be to express six of the universal emotions (anger, disgust, fear, happiness, sadness, and surprise) in eight different social situations: alone, with family, with friends, with casual acquaintances, in public, with people of lower status than oneself, with people of higher status than oneself, and with children. This study was important not only because it was the first cross-cultural study of display rules since Friesen's (1972) original study but also because it surveyed display rule attitudes across most of the universal emotions in a variety of social situations; Friesen's original study of 1972 has documented display rule differences between the American and Japanese on only a few emotions in one social situation.

The data produced some interesting, and unexpected, findings. For example, the Americans and Japanese did not differ in the degree to which they believed it was appropriate to express anger, disgust, sadness, fear, and surprise when alone. The lack of cultural differences for these emotions when alone points to the fact that this situation requires no modification of the expression; thus, no cultural differences. But the Americans rated disgust and sadness more acceptable with close friends and family members, and with children; the Japanese rated anger and fear more appropriate with casual acquaintances and in public, and they also rated anger more appropriate with people of lower status than oneself, and fear more appropriate with people of higher status than oneself.

These findings make it clear, first of all, that the Japanese are not suppressed, emotionless robots; depending on the social situation, they display more emotion than Americans do. But cultural differences in display rules help the Japanese to control and modify their emotional expressions under certain circumstances. The data are quite clear in indicating that the Americans and Japanese have quite different display rules, but not that the Japanese show no emotions at all.

Second, the pattern of findings we obtained corresponds to the nature of display rules as dictated by the Japanese culture and society. For example, the Japanese rated disgust and sadness as less appropriate than the Americans with close friends and family members because these emotions can threaten the close social bonds that exist between members of these groups. Because of the Japanese culture's emphasis on group functioning and ingroup harmony, it is important that any emotions that may threaten tightness or cohesion be discouraged.

On the other hand, the Japanese rated anger and fear more appropriate with casual acquaintances and in public. Because the situations that arouse such emotions are basically beyond individual control, display of these emotions helps to differentiate between acceptable and unacceptable groups and situations. Again, this plays an important function in maintaining the emphasis on groups in Japan. It is obvious that the higher rating of anger by the Japanese toward people of lower status than oneself helps to maintain status differences in Japan, another important cultural dimension of the Japanese. Similarly, the higher rating by the Japanese of fear toward people of higher status helps to maintain status differences.

Clearly, display rules in Japan are a complex system that has much to do with the whole nature of Japanese culture and society. The individual Japanese must follow these rules closely in order to be accepted socially in Japan. This is, as noted, the only study of display rules in Japan since the original work in this field published in 1972, but some interesting cross-cultural research on the emotional behavior of American and Japanese infants (Bradshaw, Miyake, Campos, Kanaya, & Usui, 1990; Camras, Campos, Oster, & Bradshaw, 1990; Oster, 1990), though still in preliminary stages, may stimulate further research in the matter of display rules in Japan.

Some Speculations About Japanese Display Rules

For the present, in spite of the lack of full evidence on display rules in Japan, we do know enough about the Japanese culture, and about emotion, to develop some hypotheses, which, though necessarily speculative, may be helpful in furthering formal, systematic research. The field is ripe for this type of formal inquiry, and it promises to yield more interesting, enlightening, and provocative findings concerning the nature of display rules in Japan. Certainly, one of the goals of this book is to point out avenues of new research.

There are two general characteristics about the Japanese culture that provide a framework for speculating about Japanese display rules. The first has to do with the emphasis on collective concerns and the surrender of individual aspirations for the purpose and functioning of the group. The second has to do with the emphasis on the maintenance of status differences among members within the culture. To be sure, these two characteristics reflect values and tendencies that are reinforced in various ways as an integral part of the Japanese culture. The point I make here is that these cultural values translate to specific and concrete rules concerning the regulation of emotional behavior and expression. Generally speaking, these rules suggest that emotions must be expressed appropriately so as (1) to maintain harmony and cohesion within ingroups, and to differentiate outgroups; and (2) to maintain status differences among high-, low-, and same-status others.

The remainder of this section describes some general display principles based upon these two guiding statements. The study reported above (Matsumoto, 1991) provided some support for the validity of some of these principles, as did the original display rules study (Ekman, 1972; Friesen, 1972). Many of these must of course remain as speculations until formal studies can support or refute them, but there are many examples, based on observation, that provide some anecdotal and impressionistic support for them. Each of the principles can, and must, be developed to the point where exact display rules indicating how specific emotions are to be used in specific situations can be identified and tested. It is in the hope of spurring this interest and further study that I offer these.

THE IMPORTANCE OF COLLECTIVE EMOTION

One prominent Japanese display rule concerns the sharing of emotion—*collective emotion*. The sharing of emotional expressions and experiences serves to strengthen bonds among group members, thereby filling an important role in group functioning. If the members of one's group express happiness or joy, then one must also express this joy, as a member of the group. If the other members of one's group express anger or frustration, then one must also express the same anger and frustration, conforming to the group consensus. This is collective emotion.

Because many interpersonal relationships in Japan are group-oriented, it is easy to share collective emotions. In a Japanese business company, for example, all the employees, from the president and CEO to the part-time hourly workers, will express the same emotions in response to the ups and downs of the business world. If the company receives an award, all the employees may express satisfaction, joy, or happiness. If a particular department or section of the company receives an award, all the members of that department or section will express joy or happiness. Similarly, if the company experiences a downfall, economic or otherwise, then all the members of the company will express their sadness or dejection. If another company beats them in competition, then all the members of the company will express the same anger, resentment, and disappointment. The sharing of collective emotion is an important aspect of all Japanese groups. Individual emotional expressions must conform to the group emotion; if one's individual expressions do not conform, group harmony and solidarity are threatened. Social sanctions such as shame, ridicule, or isolation may follow.

The sharing of collective emotion is an important display rule in Japan that is closely tied to the Japanese culture. One must display the appropriate emotion even if one does not actually feel it. For example, if a member of your company or organization wins an award for being the most outstanding salesperson in the industry, you as a member of the company should display joy or happiness, sharing in the expression of group emotion along with others, even though you may in fact feel jealousy or resentment toward this person. Private feelings are kept to oneself. To some extent the same code of behavior exists in other cultures, but in Japan the sanctions against not sharing in collective emotion, of whatever sort, are great.

Groups are especially strong in Japan not only because of their solidarity in behavior and thinking but also because of the unity of their emotional responses. Emotion serves as the social glue that binds all members of the group together, sometimes whether they like it or not. When you deal with the anger of one person, you actually deal with the anger of the group to which that person belongs. The concept of emotion as social glue is closely related to Kemper's (1978) notion of emotion as being socially integrating.

THE MAINTENANCE OF GROUP HARMONY

It is important for groups in Japan to be relatively harmonious and healthy. When interacting with other members of their group, the Japanese must take particular care to ensure that this group harmony is not threatened by dangerous emotions that would destroy the peace. Anger, contempt, and disgust are particularly dangerous emotions. Over the course of time, it is only natural that situations or events occur that arouse these emotions toward other group members. For example, someone may say or do something to arouse your anger at another group member. But it would be highly inappropriate to express your anger to the other person, because the open exchange of anger would threaten group cohesion. Instead, one must learn to be stoic and suppress this anger.

Over the course of time, the Japanese, like people of other cultures but probably to a greater extent, have learned to accept many things that anger them. Regardless of what happens, one must not express anger or frustration openly. Even in approaching someone with higher status who has the ability to intervene, one is usually advised to be patient and accept the situation. If something is done, it is likely to be done on the side, after hours, out of view, to avoid the open display of anger and the confrontation that might follow, and that might lead to group dysfunction. When group infighting does occur—and sometimes it does—it can be a battle. Japanese ingroup fighting is not everyday bickering over mundane things; on the contrary, the long suppression of anger can erupt in fights that are huge and devastating. Japanese history is replete with examples of major events that erupted from large and severe ingroup fighting.

Avoiding the display of negative and dangerous emotions is not the only display rule Japanese must follow to maintain group harmony. They must also learn to preserve peace and harmony. Certainly, the sharing of collective emotions serves part of this purpose. But the Japanese learn to go beyond the simple sharing of emotion; they must learn to feign positive emotion even when they feel quite negative. For example, if one is angered but it is inappropriate to display the anger, the appropriate display rule in many situations involves patience, understanding, acceptance, and a masking of the anger with a smile. To express nothing, to have a blank expression, would be an open expression of one's anger. Thus, there are many instances where the Japanese go beyond the nonexpression of the anger truly felt and actually express the opposite. Examples such as these no doubt contributed to the belief by many that emotional expressions are specific to each culture.

INGROUP AND OUTGROUP DIFFERENTIATION

In Japan, it is important to differentiate between one's ingroup and other outgroups. It is not uncommon for the Japanese to display outright indifference or even anger, contempt, and disgust toward members of other groups, even solely on the basis of group membership. The assumption is that this serves to differentiate us from them, that is, to differentiate one's own group from others, thereby further strengthening group bonds and fostering group rivalry.

It is easy to see this kind of intergroup conflict in high school and college sports. Members of sports clubs in Japan openly express competition, indifference, and negative emotions toward members of rival sports groups, but usually only in the safety of one's own ingroup. In public, open displays of negative emotions toward others, if expressed, are not so intense. At high school baseball tournaments, or any of the other big sporting events (baseball, soccer, Judo, etc.), intergroup competition in public is often expressed vigorously through the encouragement of one's own ingroup, not necessarily through the open display of negative emotions toward outgroups or rivals.

Of course, this type of intergroup conflict and rivalry only serves to strengthen the Japanese as a whole at whatever they do. As each group tries to better the others, what happens over time is that the level of proficiency of *all* the groups as a collective whole is higher than what could have been achieved by a single group working without the rivalry. This type of healthy competition has the same effect in business as it has in sports. This aspect of intergroup competition helps make the Japanese leaders in much of what they do, such as technological and medical science, some sports, business, and the like.

This high degree of competition and the outward displays of rivalry, aggression, and other negative emotions toward members of other groups in Japan are quite the opposite of the emotional expressions dictated within one's own group. On one hand, the Japanese must learn to suppress negative and dangerous emotions toward ingroups, while on the other hand, they must learn to express them toward outgroups. This is another example of how the Japanese are seemingly full of contradictions in their behavior. If we identify these contradictions as differences in display rules given different social situations, these seemingly contradictory behaviors begin to make sense.

THE IMPORTANCE OF FUTURE RELATIONSHIPS

Not all emotional displays toward outsiders are negative and differentiating. The Japanese are very aware that if there is a possibility of future, harmonious relations with someone else, they must in no way threaten this future harmony. If there seems to be no possibility of such future relationships, then there is no need to try to establish or maintain interpersonal harmony.

Probably all non-Japanese people who have visited Japan have experienced what they perceive as great indifference and almost disrespect, but this often occurs in situations when there is no possibility of future relationships, and therefore no need for the Japanese to display emotions that foster harmony. It is not uncommon for non-Japanese to comment that the Japanese are racial bigots because of the offhand ways in which they treat outsiders. Though it is difficult to confirm such comments objectively, it is important to keep them in perspective. The Japanese can, and do, treat other Japanese people the same way—witness the behavior on the commute trains at rush hour in Tokyo, Osaka, and other major cities. What non-Japanese perceive as racism or discrimination of some sort or other happens among the Japanese all the time: people push and pull others ferociously, and they pay little attention to those with special needs or concerns (handicapped, pregnant women, people with baggage, etc.). The question is really how one's own cultural expectations and background color one's perceptions of these events. My guess would be that the Japanese do not perceive many of these acts as discriminatory at all.

If there is a possibility of future relationship, however, Japanese display rules dictate a great concern and caring for interpersonal relationships. The Japanese will go out of their way to establish and maintain personal relationships and harmony. Politeness takes precedent. Anger and other negative and dangerous emotions are suppressed, and masked by smiles, all of which can be a façade to maintain harmonious relationships. The business world is notorious for these façades. Salespeople must smile and be infinitely patient with customers, for the business depends on future relationships with them. (Just ask any insurance or real estate agent dealing with a Japanese market.) Business interactions with the Japanese are often marked by politeness, acceptance, and tolerance, so much so that it is often quite difficult to gauge exactly where the other side stands.

Entrance into new groups is often difficult, for Japanese and non-Japanese alike. Anyone who enters a new group will be treated with politeness but also with caution and indifference, perhaps for a long time—or until the new member proves himself worthy of group membership by showing allegiance. Only after the new member has passed the test will other group members treat him or her like a true member of the group. Politeness and harmony, though agreeable at the start of a relationship, may take on other meanings if they are prolonged. When this happens, the message may be that one really is not yet a full-fledged member of the group. Many non-Japanese complain that others are still so polite to them after so many years that they know they are still looked upon as an outsider.

Again, many of these apparent contradictions in Japanese behavior can be interpreted as differences in display rules as they apply to different social situations. These rules of engagement are necessary to perpetuate and maintain ingroup vs. outgroup differences. Emotion, and its expression, will serve as the social marker for continuing to differentiate between oneself and one's group with other groups and people.

DEFERENCE TO HIGHER-STATUS OTHERS

The Japanese culture emphasizes status differences to a great degree, and encourages its members to display only those emotions that serve to maintain the status differences that exist between interactants. Toward someone of higher status, one must always display (or not display, depending on the situation) emotions that reinforce the difference in status. This principle was at work in Ekman and Friesen's original study on display rules. When the Japanese participants viewed the stressful films in the presence of a higher-status experimenter, they modified their facial behaviors to display smiles even though the films elicited disgust, fear, and anger. Clearly, the Japanese have a display rule that dictates the suppression of negative emotions to higher-status others, and the masking of these emotions with smiles. To have expressed these negative emotions in the presence of the experimenter would have been contrary to the display rule, upsetting the status differences between the interactants. For example, the expression of negative emotions by the participants in that situation might have put them psychologically on an equivalent status level with the experimenter, which would be unacceptable to the cultural emphasis on maintaining status differences.

In everyday interaction in Japan, this display rule is particularly noticeable when anger is aroused toward someone of higher status than oneself. If a boss (higher status), for example, does not recognize an employee (lower status) for a job well done, or if the boss is angry at the employee, the employee generally has no recourse but to accept the indifference or anger. In the Japanese culture, it is not the employee's place to challenge the boss's anger by showing one's own anger, however much that emotion is aroused and regardless of how much resentment one feels. One must accept the blame or indifference and anger, often with sincerity and apology. This does not mean that the employee will not feel angry: indeed, the employee may feel downright outraged at the boss, or at the people who really should be blamed, or both, or at the whole company. But the Japanese display rule dictates that the employee cannot show this anger to the boss, especially in public. The employee must accept the blame with outward sincerity, even if he or she feels like wringing the boss's neck.

If the employee did show anger, even in the slightest degree, the employee would in effect be putting him or herself on an equal footing with the boss. In the United States and other cultures that place less emphasis on status, people will comment on how terrible it is that they must endure such unfairness. In the individualistic American culture, people are taught to speak their mind; if others, no matter who, become angry, and if they are wrong, one learns to stand up for one's rights and attempt to correct mistakes. It would also not be uncommon for American employees to demand a public apology from the boss. In Japan, this would be one of the most shameful experiences for the boss, company, and even the employee. The root of this American-Japanese difference is the degree to which both cultures foster status differentiation. American culture minimizes status differences, emphasizing equality among people, regardless of actual differences in status or power. The Japanese culture maintains status differences, and incorporates rituals and rules to maintain these differences.

There are other times, of course, when one must show deference to higher-status others that do not involve such intense negative emotions. Many times, for example, one must feign positive emotion to satisfy the status differential that exists between oneself and a higher-status other. There are many other instances where lower-status persons must show deference in their emotional behavior to higher-status others.

THE MAINTENANCE OF ONE'S OWN HIGH STATUS

The Japanese culture's emphasis on status difference does not, however, mean that rules exist only for people of lower status; those of higher status must also follow strict cultural display rules that govern their emotional behavior. Higher-status people must behave in ways that maintain status differentials. For example, it is more acceptable for a higher-status person to display anger toward lower-status others than vice versa, and the ability of a higher-status person to display anger toward lower-status others maintains, if not accentuates, the status differences. Lower-status persons do not have the same privilege. The higher-status Japanese must also be careful not to show emotions that may be interpreted as signs of weakness. (Indeed, the display of anger is one manifestation of this rule.) A group leader who feels sadness or fear must take care to suppress those feelings, perhaps by remaining emotionless and calm. If leaders display emotions such as sadness or fear inappropriately, they can be judged as weak, and perhaps unfitting as a leader. This would reduce the status differential that existed between the leader and the followers.

Japanese display rules also dictate that persons of higher status should be cautious in showing the emotions of joy and happiness. Japanese leaders frequently remain absolutely expressionless when they, or the people below them, achieve something. In the sports world, it is not uncommon for a Japanese player or teams who have just won a major championship to be greeted by a simple nod of acknowledgment by the coach, or even by tears, even though everyone else may be panicked with happiness. Outbursts of joy by the participants may be appropriate (but *not too* much); but similar outbursts by the coach or team leaders are not appropriate. Showing such emotion places them on an even footing with the rest of the team, and that minimizes the status differences that exist.

A corollary to these display rules for persons of higher status is the underlying Japanese philosophy that, in order to be able to endure intense, emotional events of life, one must learn to resist the temptation to become emotional about them—to have inner strength. The control of one's emotions is central to achieving a higher status in the Japanese way of thinking. Differences in the degree of control will often differentiate between persons of high and low status. Furthermore, the pressure to control one's emotions becomes greater the higher status one achieves. Inappropriate emotional displays are tolerated more with lower-status people, and are often attributed to youth or inexperience. As one gains experience, and correspondingly status, the pressure on controlling one's emotions increases. Careful control of one's emotions indicates that one is becoming a stronger person, and leader. In this sense, emotional control is intimately related to maturity in Japan; maturity, in turn, is related to status and age, because status often comes with age.

Controlling one's emotions does not necessarily mean suppressing emotions. Rather, it means that persons of higher status must be able to display emotions appropriately. For example, leaders must, in appropriate situations, show compassion and understanding for lower-status people under them. At other times, it means that one must sincerely show gratitude, respect, and appreciation. Sometimes being of a higher status means that one must have the ability to humble oneself in ways that others cannot, especially to subordinates. By displaying these sorts of emotions appropriately, persons of higher status inspire loyalty and respect from their subordinates.

In Japan, it is generally not good to act "too much" like a person with status. The saying, "the higher (status) one becomes, the lower one must bow," captures the essence of what is demanded of one who is of a higher status. Being of a higher status in Japan demands that one weigh and act upon numerous display rules that present conflicting necessities in terms of emotional regulation and control.

The Primary Emotion Mask: The Smile

Lafcadio Hearn, the English-educated Irish-Greek writer who spent the last fourteen years of his life in Japan (1890–1904) and wrote several books on his adopted country, wrote perceptively of the Japanese smile:

A Japanese can smile in the face of death, and usually does. But he then smiles for the same reason that he smiles at other times. There is neither defiance nor hypocrisy in the smile; nor is it to be confounded with that smile of sickly resignation which we are apt to associate with weakness of character. It is an elaborate and long-cultivated etiquette. It is also a silent language. But any effort to interpret it according to Western notions of physiognomical expression would be just about as successful as an attempt to interpret Chinese ideographs by their real or fancied resemblance to shapes of familiar things.

. . . The stranger cannot fail to notice the generally happy and smiling character of the native faces; and this first impression is, in most cases, wonderfully pleasant. The Japanese smile at first charms. It is only at a later day, when one has observed the same smile under extraordinary circumstances— in moments of pain, shame, disappointment—that one becomes suspicious of it. Its apparent inopportuneness may even, on certain occasions, cause violent anger. Indeed, many of the difficulties between foreign residents and their native servants have been due to the smile.

. . . The smile is taught like the bow, like the prostration. . . . But the smile is to be used upon all pleasant occasions, when speaking to a superior or to an equal, and even upon occasions which are not pleasant; it is part of deportment. The most agreeable face is the smiling face; and to present always the most agreeable face possible to parents, relatives, teachers, friends, well-wishers, is a rule of life. . . . Even though the heart is breaking, it is a social duty to smile bravely. (Hearn, 1894, pp. 658–59)

When Japanese mask or conceal emotions, the expression most often used is the smile. This was observed in Ekman and Friesen's (1972) original study where Japanese participants smiled in the presence of a higher-status experimenter to hide their intense, negative feelings. Many other instances point to the fact that smile is not only a sign of true pleasure or joy; it can also be a sign of acceptance, resignation, or tolerance of a situation. Actually, the use of a smile as an emotion qualifier or mask is not limited to the Japanese. The smile is widely used for similar purposes in a variety of situations, contexts, and cultures. Ekman (1985) and Ekman and Friesen (1982) outline a number of different ways in which the smile can be used, cutting across cultural boundaries.

Some expressions are very difficult to produce voluntarily. The smile is perhaps one of the easiest. Everyone (with the exception of patients with neurological damage to the facial nerve or other areas of the brain regulating facial control) can voluntarily innervate the muscle used in the smile to pull the corners of the lips up (zygomatic major). The degree of neural control of the smile expression, and the messages that usually accompany it, make the smile a most versatile expression.

The smile of genuine joy or happiness is different from the qualifying or masking smile. When smiles are used to feign positive emotion, the configuration usually lacks the innervation of the muscle surrounding the eye—orbicularis oculi. Ekman and his colleagues have recently coined the term "Duchenne's smile" to denote smiles signaling truly felt happiness, and have reported data substantiating the differences between these and other types of smiles (Ekman, Davidson, & Friesen, 1990). Our work also suggests that with some training, one can become quite proficient in discriminating between smiles signaling genuine feelings of happiness or joy and smiles used to mask one's true feelings.

Because of the degree to which display rules are important in the Japanese culture, smiles take on added importance. The Japanese clearly do not harbor the same attitudes and beliefs about the smile that non-Japanese (e.g., Americans) do. Many of these differences have been substantiated in our research on emotional perception, which will be discussed in a later chapter.

Emotional Display and Experience:
Primary and Secondary Emotions

This chapter has dealt with how the Japanese culture influences emotional behavior or expressions by means of display rules. We have focused primarily on rules of the facial display of emotion. Because emotion is expressed primarily in the face, and because the face is a source of so much information in normal social interaction, it is only natural that most of the effects of Japanese cultural display rules be centered on controlling what happens on the face. But it is important to remember that cultural display rules affect the display of emotion, and not necessarily one's inner, emotional experience. Suppressing the display of anger, for example, does not necessarily mean that one's feelings of anger are completely suppressed. It may very well be the case that one's face is neutral or smiling to conceal the anger that one truly feels inside. The face can, and does, show one thing even though one feels something entirely different, and this is true for any of the universal emotions.

The conflict between what one feels and what one shows in the Japanese culture highlights the distinction of what I call *primary* and *secondary* emotions. Primary emotions are the emotions that one experiences naturally in reaction to emotion-eliciting events. Secondary emotions are those that one experiences in reaction to the primary emotion. Both primary and secondary emotions are important in the Japanese culture; secondary emotions are especially important in understanding the individual Japanese. For example, if one is angry toward someone of higher status, we know that it would probably be inappropriate for this anger to be expressed, because of the emphasis in Japanese culture on status differentiation and its corresponding display rules. The primary emotion in this case is clearly anger. But the fact that one is experiencing anger without being able to express it adequately may lead to another emotional reaction. This is the secondary emotion.

In a certain situation, for example, some people might resign themselves to the need for having to accept the higher-status person's anger; their secondary emotion might be sadness. Another person in the same situation might actually become afraid, experiencing fear in reaction either to the higher-status person's anger or to one's own anger, or both. Another person might experience disgust at both the situation, the higher-status person, and perhaps even toward oneself. Yet another person might become even more frustrated and angry at the whole situation. These are all examples of possible secondary emotions. They are secondary because they are all reactions to the original (primary) emotion that started the chain of emotions and display rules (in this example, anger). The existence of secondary emotions makes the social obligations of Japanese people that much more difficult because they must deal with the regulation and control not only of the primary emotion but also of the secondary emotion.

To be sure, the original display rule concept was intended to explain cultural differences in the expression of primary, not secondary, emotions. The existence and exact nature of secondary emotions, and their corresponding display rules, need to be corroborated by formal studies examining these ideas. My guess is that investigation of secondary emotional reactions on the part of the Japanese would yield a rich and wonderfully complex set of findings that could tell us even more about their emotional lives. There is every indication to suggest that secondary emotional reactions are real, and important, but that they lack the same degree and precision of formalized display rules of primary emotional reactions. Although the Japanese people may appear to be either emotionless or emotional robots, nothing could be further from the truth; in most cases where a primary emotion is elicited and a Japanese display rule prevents its expression, the person is most likely experiencing different, intense emotions, often negative.

Individual Variations in Japanese Emotional Behavior

All cultures have display rules, and on some theoretical levels, they all serve the same purpose, that is, of providing guidelines for individual members to maintain the culture. What differentiates the Japanese culture and individual Japanese from non-Japanese is not that these rules exist, but rather the degree to which they exist. The Japanese culture depends in large measure on the strict adherence by all members to display rules, like other cultural rituals and social institutions. Stiff sanctions exist for transgression of these rules, and those who do not conform must expect shame, ridicule, or isolation. Indeed, many native Japanese believe that one cannot be considered a "full-fledged" Japanese until one has mastered the art of managing one's emotions in all aspects of life.

The degree to which the Japanese culture fosters these rules, and to which the Japanese people follow these rules, leaves very little room for individual variation. Given the arousal of a certain emotion in a certain situation and context, many Japanese will behave in exactly the same ways, according to the display rule governing that emotion and situation. In contrast, in individualistic societies such as that of the United States, people respond in different ways to the same emotion and situation. American society tolerates, and to a great extent fosters, a wide range of emotional behavior, even though display rules exist. Americans are also more tolerant of transgression of these rules. The Japanese are not, resulting in conformity and uniformity in the application of rules in Japanese social behavior.

Still, the high degree of conformity in Japanese emotional behavior and adherence to display rules does not mean that individual variation does not exist. It merely suggests that we must look elsewhere for individual differences. One good place to start is in the area of secondary emotions. Perhaps owing to the lack of formalized display rules governing secondary emotions, the Japanese seem to display a wide range of individual expression of secondary emotions, which, though they may be inappropriate in many instances, often occur in situations in which their expression is unsanctioned.

Another area in which Japanese individual differences can be considered is that of subjective emotional experience. The fact that there is a difference between emotional displays and experience allows the Japanese some room for individuality, and it is in the inner workings of one's emotional life that individual differences among the Japanese can be observed, despite uniformity of facial response.

Chapter 4

Emotions on the Inside

The Subjective Experiences of the Japanese

Although facial expressions and cultural display rules are extremely important in understanding the emotions of the Japanese people, they only tell part of the story of their emotional life. Emotion is a package of separate but interrelated components. One of these is emotional expression. The others, equally important, are the subjective experience or feeling of emotion, physiological arousal and sensations, antecedents and elicitors of emotion, and the perception of emotion in others. For a full understanding of the emotional life of the Japanese, we must examine these aspects of emotions as well. Our research program has done just that, and in this chapter we turn our attention to the subjective experience of emotion.

Previous works that have focused on the subjective emotional experience of the Japanese have for the most part centered on the emotion of shame, and its corresponding emotion of guilt (e.g., Lebra, 1976; Doi, 1973). Certainly, these emotions are very important and real in the emotional life of the Japanese, and they have generally been understood in relation to transgressions on group or social norms, and the corresponding context and situation within which these emotions are elicited. Given the emphasis within the Japanese culture on social norms and group functioning, it is only natural that these two emotions deserve special consideration in the Japanese culture.

Still, there are many other types of emotional reactions that the Japanese, and people of any culture, can have. The last two chapters showed how the emotions of anger, contempt, disgust, fear, happiness, sadness, and surprise are all universally expressed, and how cultural display rules can modify their expression. Because these emotions are profoundly important to human functioning, we have broadened our conceptual and empirical horizons to encompass them.

Examination of the inner emotional experiences of the Japanese has important practical implications. The myth of Japanese inscrutability, long held by scholars and laypersons alike, has its foundation in observations of display rules that dictate the neutralizing of emotional expressions in social contexts—on outward appearance, in other words—and it has been assumed that lack of expression of emotion means that no emotion is felt. Now that we have learned more about display rules, it makes sense to probe seriously the subjective experiences of the Japanese. Indeed, the existence of display rules makes it all the more imperative to examine emotions on the inside—to investigate how and when the Japanese experience all emotions, not just shame and guilt, and how their experiences may or may not be different from those of non-Japanese. That is, because culture can influence the management of emotional expression, it becomes equally plausible that subjective emotional experience is also managed as a function of culture.

This chapter presents findings from our research program examining the emotional experiences of the Japanese. Though many questions still await further research, the findings from these studies make it clear that the Japanese, like any other people, have a rich and marvelously varied inner emotional life, even if the expression of these emotions is regulated and often neutralized. Moreover, we now understand that, owing to the many demands that are made on the Japanese people in terms of the regulation of their outside emotional expressions, their inside emotional life can be highly complex, and often confusing.

In our studies of the inner emotional life of the Japanese people, we have looked at a range of emotions, and we have tried to be comprehensive in our coverage about different dimensions or aspects of the experiences. The data we have obtained indicate the frequency, intensity, and duration of emotional experience, and they also assess the verbal, nonverbal, and physiological sensations as reactions to emotion-eliciting situations, and the degree to which the Japanese attempt to control or regulate these.

Each of these dimensions can be related to stereotypical notions about the inner emotional lives of the Japanese. For example, because of the existence of Japanese display rules to neutralize or mask the expression of one's true feelings, one might expect the Japanese to experience emotions less frequently, less intensely, and for shorter durations, than non-Japanese (e.g., Americans). Similar expectations, or hypotheses, based on our knowledge of display rules and our stereotypical notions of the Japanese, can be produced on the other dimensions of emotion as well. These will be discussed in more detail within each specific section below. Assessment of the subjective experience of the Japanese along these dimensions makes it possible to test whether or not these expectations are correct.

Two studies in particular inform us about the subjective experience of emotion in the Japanese. In one study (Scherer, Matsumoto, Wallbott, & Kudoh, 1988), we compared the responses of a sample of Japanese respondents with comparable samples in Europe and the United States, who all reported their reactions to events that elicited anger, fear, happiness, and sadness in them. In a second study (Matsumoto, Kudoh, Scherer, & Wallbott, 1988), we compared the responses of a sample of Japanese respondents with an American sample who reported their experiences of anger, fear, happiness, sadness, disgust, guilt, and shame. Both studies were conducted as a part of large cross-cultural surveys on the subjective experience of emotion that involved over 3,000 subjects in over 30 different countries (Matsumoto, Wallbott, & Scherer, in preparation; Scherer, Wallbott, & Summerfield, 1986; Wallbott & Scherer, 1986). These findings suggest that the inner emotional life of the Japanese is a rich, complex, and exciting area of their lives, and is no less important to them than it would be to any other people of the world. Moreover, many of the specific findings are in direct contrast to our expectations about the subjective experiences of the Japanese.

The Emotional Experiences of the Japanese

THE FREQUENCY OF EMOTIONAL EXPERIENCE

When we conducted our research in Japan, we asked the respondents to tell us about their emotional experiences, and how long ago they had occurred. Stereotypical notions about the Japanese would suggest that they tend to ignore or neglect their emotional experiences, and we therefore expected the Japanese to report that their emotional experiences occurred much further in the past than their American or European counterparts. On the contrary, we found just the opposite. For each emotion we studied, the Japanese reported that their emotional experiences occurred more recently than those of the Americans or Europeans.

These findings suggested to us several possibilities about Japanese emotional experiences, all contrary to traditional, stereotypical notions. First, these findings suggested that each of the emotions occurred with greater frequency for the Japanese than for the Europeans or Americans. The Japanese experience emotions more often than we believe. Second, these findings suggested that the Japanese place greater prominence on their emotions than do non-Japanese: they think more about their emotions, keep them in their minds longer, and place greater importance on them than do non-Japanese.

These ideas are interesting in the context of interpersonal relationships in Japan, whether between other ingroup members or between people of differing status. It would appear that the Japanese cultural emphasis on interpersonal relationships means that emotions are more easily aroused, and that the Japanese place more emphasis on emotions when they occur because they have meaning for future relations. In other words, the Japanese, unlike Americans and Europeans, view emotional events within a framework that involves other people in a stream of events across time.

This Japanese view of emotional experience is in contrast to the traditional view of emotion in American psychology, which views emotion as a single, discrete event that is of primary importance to one person in a single context, place, and time. Western culture and society focus less on interpersonal relationships, and more on the individual. Emotional events, when they occur, are considered private, personal, and independent, not necessarily connected to any future relationships. Thus, there is less emphasis placed on emotions as they occur within a stream of events over time. One can say that in Americans, emotions have meaning for the self, and in Japanese, for self-other relationships.

Even though the average Japanese must go to great lengths to manage overt displays of emotion via display rules, these data suggest that emotion is really on the mind for Japanese much more than for non-Japanese, and certainly more than non-Japanese believe. For the Japanese, the emotions that have occurred in the past have direct relevance for interpersonal relationships today; similarly, the emotions that occur today will affect the relationships of tomorrow.

THE INTENSITY AND DURATION OF EMOTIONAL EXPERIENCE

In both our studies, we asked the respondents to tell us how long they experienced the emotions when they occurred (duration), and how strongly they felt them (intensity). Stereotype would suggest that the Japanese really don't feel emotions very strongly at all, or for very long, that they dismiss their emotions as if they were not important or were undesirable.

Once again, the data surprised us. When compared against the American samples, the Japanese did report that they felt the emotions for shorter periods of time, and with less intensity. However, there was no difference between what the Japanese respondents told us and what their European counterparts said. Also, when we examined the actual scale values that were used in obtaining the responses, it was clear that the Japanese tended to report on the high end of the scale rather than the low.

These findings indicated that the Japanese do indeed feel emotions quite intensely and for considerable periods of time. The fact that there were no differences between the Japanese and European respondents stands in direct contradiction to Western stereotypes of the Japanese feeling emotions less intensely or for shorter durations than Westerners. The Americans had higher ratings than the Japanese, but an equally plausible interpretation of this difference may be that Americans exaggerate their ratings when assessing their emotional states using scales. In the absence of data to suggest otherwise, it is impossible to decide which interpretation is correct.

These findings are especially interesting when we consider the effect of display rules on emotional expressions of the Japanese. The Japanese people must go out of their way to manage, mask, conceal, or modify their emotional expressions so as not to show what they truly feel. This aspect of the Japanese culture and individual behavior has suggested that the Japanese do not feel emotions, especially when considered in light of traditional American psychological notions of the intimate relationship between expression and experience. The data provided in these studies with Japanese respondents challenge this traditional point of view in so far as they indicate that the Japanese experience emotions quite intensely, even though they may not show them as readily as non-Japanese.

But what happens to those intense feelings that are not being expressed? The answer probably lies in the distinction between primary and secondary emotions. Because we did not assess secondary emotions in these studies, we can only speculate about how the Japanese experience them. Japanese people are often caught in a bind: on one hand, they are feeling emotions just as intensely and for the same amount of time as anyone else is; on the other, they cannot show many of these emotions sincerely or directly. This bind can produce feelings of frustration, anger, or resentment—toward the situation, toward one's inability to express (and thus release) one's emotions, toward "being Japanese." On the other hand, the bind can result in feelings of remorse and resignation in response to the fact that they really cannot express their feelings freely, and that that is merely the "way it is"; nothing can change the system.

Japanese culture and society do, however, provide for some release of these controlled emotions. After-hours socializing plays an especially important role in Japanese culture; it allows people to loosen up, and to release frustrations built up from the day's events and express their individuality. After hours, when the rules of Japanese culture are relaxed, people can be more themselves. There is yet another benefit to this ritual in that the sharing of the release of the emotions that accrue during the day serves to strengthen further the bonds between people, and this in turn further strengthens group solidarity and harmony. Very likely one of the reasons that non-Japanese, including researchers, have long regarded the Japanese people as emotionless is that they have been barred from intimate society where they could observe this side of the Japanese emotionality.

Another interesting cultural institution related to the release of emotion is the sometimes exaggerated expression of emotions in the arts of the Japanese culture. Japanese literature, for example, is replete with many commentaries of one sort and another on Japanese culture and society, with an underlying current of frustration toward the "system." This message can be inferred clearly from works as early as *Genji Monogatari* (The Tale of Genji) and *Makura no Soushi* (The Pillow Book), through Saikaku, Tanizaki, and Mishima. One of the most popular classic Japanese films is *Otoko wa Tsurai Yo*, which concerns the unfortunate life of one nonconformist Japanese man in a society that refuses to tolerate his nonconformism.

It comes as no surprise to those who are familiar with the Japanese culture and people, including the Japanese themselves, that the Japanese experience emotions with great intensity and for considerable periods of time. The Japanese accept the rules, but they are not fooled by outward appearances, or by the lack of such appearances. They learn to understand and appreciate the unspoken, unexpressed, subjective emotional experiences of others solely on the basis of the situation, of knowing who the players are, what their relationship is, and what happened. In this way, the Japanese are able to empathize with others in ways that are difficult for non-Japanese. This is one of the truly unique aspects of Japanese emotional life that not only exists but flourishes unnoticed by the untrained eye, and is often beyond the perceptions of Western scientists.

VERBAL AND NONVERBAL REACTIONS

Ample research has documented the fact that the Japanese differ from non-Japanese in their overt expressions because of cultural display rules; but are the Japanese actually *aware* of the fact that their reactions and expressions are different? The extent to which people realize that they are controlling their emotional displays raises important theoretical and practical questions about the relationship between learning, rules, and behavior. In adults, many display rules governing emotional behavior are adhered to automatically, which may imply that display rules are outside conscious awareness.

When asked, will the Japanese report that their reactions are different, and that they are consciously trying to control or regulate their reactions? We asked the respondents in our surveys to tell us about their verbal, nonverbal, and physiological reactions when they experienced their emotions. We thought it was important to ask not only about their outside, observable, behavioral reactions (speech, yelling, facial expressions, gestures, body movements, etc.) but also about inner, physical reactions that cannot be seen. Would the Japanese report that sensations of their physiological events concur with observable behaviors? Or would the Japanese report a negative relationship between inside and outside?

Without qualification, the Japanese reported less activity on both the inside and the outside. They reported less verbalization, less expressive behavior, and fewer physiological sensations than their American and European counterparts. For example, the Japanese had fewer speech utterances, fewer conversations about their reactions, fewer facial reactions, less gazing, fewer hand or body movements, fewer feelings of temperature changes, heartbeat differences, stomach or gastrointestinal changes. This picture is consistent with stereotypical notions of the Japanese and with other studies on display rules and facial expressions of emotion. What is amazing about these data, however, is that the Japanese reported fewer of all these reactions even though their reports of subjective, inner emotional experiences were very little different from those of the Americans and Europeans. The overall picture suggests that people of different cultural backgrounds can differ drastically on the outside even though their inner emotional experiences are quite similar.

We also asked the respondents how consciously they tried to control or regulate their emotional reactions. We believed that the Japanese would report that they exerted a much greater degree of control and regulation over their emotional reactions than did the non-Japanese. We were wrong again. We found no difference in the degree to which the Japanese said they controlled their verbal or nonverbal expressive reactions, or physiological symptoms and sensations, compared with the Americans and Europeans. Although one could interpret these findings to mean that the Japanese do not regulate their emotions, another interpretation is more plausible: that the Japanese have learned to modify their emotional reactions so well, and from such an early age, that as adults their reaction patterns are automatic with little conscious effort. By the time they are adults, though they may not realize it, they have learned to control almost every aspect of external, physical reaction to emotions.

In retrospect, this is really no surprise at all. Cultural display rules governing the expression of emotion, regardless of channel or modality, should be sufficiently internalized by the time we are adults. In fact, our notion that the Japanese are controlling their emotional expressions is in itself a culturally biased view of how the Japanese handle their emotions. We only view it as control because we view it from a bias to express freely; the Japanese will not view it as control *as much* because it is simply part of being Japanese, part of their normal lives.

Altogether, these studies show quite clearly that the inner emotional life of the Japanese is not at all devoid of emotion or feeling but is on the contrary a rich, complex, and meaningful part of their lives. The Japanese experience emotions more frequently, more intensely, and for longer periods than we expected. Although the Japanese did report less in the way of verbal and nonverbal reactions and physiological sensations, there was no difference in the degree to which they attempted to exert conscious or deliberate control over these reactions and sensations.

In spite of the almost exclusive emphasis on shame and guilt by earlier writers, these are definitely not the only emotions that the Japanese experience, nor are they the only emotions that are important in the Japanese culture and society. Anger, contempt, disgust, fear, happiness, sadness, and surprise—the same emotions that are important to people of all cultures—are just as important in the normal, everyday lives of the Japanese. Although there may be cultural differences between Japanese and non-Japanese in the meaning and importance of emotions such as shame and guilt, there are many similarities—as well as differences—in their experience of the other emotions.

These findings must be considered in relation to our discussion of emotional expression. Regardless of what is happening on the level of expression, we cannot be fooled into believing that subjective, emotional experience on the inside is not occurring, or that it is not important to the Japanese. The findings summarized here indicate clearly that this is simply not the case. Perhaps no one knows this better than the Japanese themselves. The Japanese tend to rely on subtle, nonverbal cues to understanding the emotions of other Japanese, as well as on information about the situation and context of behavior. They place much more emphasis on what is unspoken or unexpressed than on what is said, at the same time placing a high value on empathizing with the emotional experiences of others. The

Japanese themselves are not fooled into thinking that emotions are dormant on the inside by what may or may not be occurring on the outside.

Understanding the Similarities and Differences in the Subjective, Emotional Experiences of the Japanese: Feeling Rules

The Japanese are both similar to and different from Americans and Europeans in their subjective experiences of emotion. I believe that there are both universal and culturally specific aspects to emotional experience, just as there are universal and culturally relative aspects to emotional expression. There really is no question about the fact that the Japanese are very emotional. The important question for theory and future research is which aspects of experience are culturally universal, and which are not.

Clearly, the fact that the Japanese have intense and meaningful emotional experiences is in itself a universal phenomenon. This may seem to be a common-sensical notion, particularly after considering all the data we have amassed about their experiences, but it is in contrast to stereotypes of the Japanese. Emotion is a universal phenomenon, and the Japanese have many of the same kinds of emotional reactions, with the same kinds of subjective feelings, as people in all parts of the world. On a theoretical level, the subjective experience of emotion has the meaning for the Japanese as it does for non-Japanese. That is, emotions serve as the social glue of the Japanese society and culture. The sharing of emotions, the release and control of emotion and its expression, and the nonverbal, subtle degrees of empathy that occur in relation to the emotional experiences of others all serve to maintain the close-knit and strongly interpersonal nature of the Japanese society. Yet though this role of emotion may be universal, how this is accomplished in the Japanese culture, or in any culture, points to how emotions can also be culturally specific, unique to a single culture or society. For the Japanese, the social and interpersonal strengthening of bonds with ingroup others, and the distinguishing between ingroup and outgroup others, are accomplished through the strict regulation of emotional expression.

In considering the specific ways by which cultures regulate subjective emotional experience, Arlie Hochshild from the University of California at Berkeley has coined a particularly useful term, "feeling rules." Although she developed this term in reference to more sociologically oriented views of emotion and the consequences to health, the concept of feeling rules can be easily applied to understanding cultural differences in emotional experience. Feeling rules are cultur-

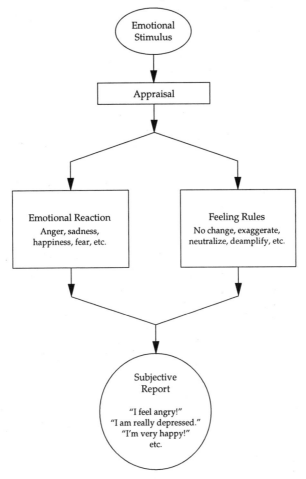

Fig. 3. A Process Model of Emotional Experience Activation Involving Culturally Learned Feeling Rules

ally and socially derived rules that govern when and how one can experience emotion. Like display rules, they are most likely learned early in life, and in the individual Japanese become an automatic, subconscious part of personal conduct. The fact that the Japanese did not report that they controlled or regulated their emotional experiences, even though they clearly had less response on both the outside and inside, points to the degree to which feeling rules can become so automatic that they do not require any conscious control or decision.

Future cross-cultural research and theorizing on subjective emotional experience will most likely find it useful to include the concept of feeling rules. A tentative model of how the Japanese experience emotions may resemble the process outlined in Figure 3. In this model, an emotion-eliciting stimulus is perceived and evaluated in terms of its relationship to the person's well-being. On the basis of this appraisal process, an appropriate emotion will be triggered. But this message is mediated by culturally learned feeling rules, which may act to modify the original emotion message. The resulting experience of emotion therefore represents the interactive product of individual cognitive appraisal of emotion-eliciting stimuli and culturally learned feeling rules.

This model of emotion activation is similar to a general model of emotion elicitation involving cognitive appraisal processes ascribed to by a number of emotion theorists, including Lazarus (1966), Leventhal (1984), and Scherer (1984). Not everyone agrees on the question of how much cognitive processing is necessary to elicit certain emotional reactions (e.g., see Zajonc, 1980), but these models of emotion are generally accepted in psychology. Little has been said, however, about the degree to which culturally learned rules affect this process, and exactly where in the process the effect occurs. Future research will need to address this question.

Primary and Secondary Emotions

The last chapter discussed the importance of making a distinction between primary and secondary emotions. As with research on emotional expression, all the cross-cultural research presented above concerning the subjective emotional experience of the Japanese has focused on primary emotional reactions. Because our research has only attempted to assess the initial reactions that the respondents may have had in relation to emotion-eliciting situations, the data concerning frequency, intensity, duration, verbal and nonverbal reactions, physiological sensations, and control, describe primary emotional reactions.

However, although it has been necessary for us to examine primary emotions in this detail, I believe that the emotional lives of the Japanese are especially varied and complex at the level of secondary emotions. The strength of Japanese display rules governing the expression of primary emotions will produce considerable secondary emotional reactions. In addition, the existence of Japanese feeling rules governing the subjective experience of emotion calls forth the importance of secondary emotional reactions even further.

Secondary emotions must be more important and salient in the Japanese culture than in a culture like the American culture, which has fewer cultural and social pressures to control primary emotional reactions. Americans will care less than Japanese about cultural display or feeling rules, and certainly not so intensely. But if Americans exhibit considerable individual variation in primary emotional response, there is probably not so much individual variation in their secondary emotional responses. For the Japanese, the opposite will occur: there is very little individual variation in primary emotional responses, but there will be relatively greater individual differences in secondary emotional reactions.

Some readers may draw similarities between primary and secondary emotions and the concepts of *tatemae* and *honne*, which refer generally to the difference between what Japanese show on the outside for social appearances (*tatemae*) and what they truly feel (*honne*). The concepts are very important in the Japanese culture and have been discussed thoroughly in the past (e.g., Doi, 1985). They are, however, different from the distinction between primary and secondary emotions. A Japanese person may show and feel an emotion that is socially appropriate (*tatemae*) even though he or she truly feels something else (*honne*); the existence of secondary emotions suggests another level of emotional complexity. Secondary emotional reactions are emotions that occur as a result of their *honne* being unexpressed. This reaction occurs above and beyond their initial *honne* and *tatemae* reactions. *Tatemae* and *honne* describe the difference between one's true emotional feelings and what one may show for social appropriateness, and in this sense, they are closely related to display rules. Primary and secondary emotions add yet another level of complexity to this picture.

These ideas concerning primary and secondary emotions are speculations until future research can assess their validity, but it is my hope that they will encourage a better understanding and appreciation of the subjective, emotional experiences of the Japanese, and spur new developments, and new research, into this theoretically important area of the emotions.

Chapter 5

Antecedents and Evaluations
of Emotion in Japan

Compared with the number of studies on the expression and perception of facial expressions, on the language and lexicons of emotion, and on the subjective, self-reported experience of emotion, surprisingly few cross-cultural studies have examined the antecedents or elicitors of emotion, which are, of course, crucial to the production of emotional experience. Antecedents are the events, situations, or occurrences that bring about emotional reactions. I use the terms antecedents and elicitors interchangeably. A number of interesting and relevant aspects of emotion antecedents are important to emotion. For example, one could examine what types of situations, events, or occurrences bring about emotions, or what types of meanings these events or situations hold, or how people cognitively evaluate these events or situations in their minds and how these evaluations or appraisals help to form and mold emotional experience.

This chapter examines the antecedents to emotions in Japan, and how the Japanese people evaluate them, and compares their antecedents and evaluations to those of people from the United States and Europe. As before, we will see that there are considerable areas of both similarity and difference between the Japanese and people of other cultures. The important question, therefore, is not whether they are similar or different, but in what ways the Japanese are similar, and in what ways they are different, and why these similarities and differences exist.

Scholars have historically disagreed about the relative nature of antecedent events that produce emotions. On one hand, some (e.g., Mead, 1967; Benedict, 1946) have suggested that emotion elicitors must differ across cultures. Mead and Benedict argued that the contexts in which people lived varied too greatly among cultures to allow for cultural similarity in antecedents. This point of view was also congruent with the notion that the expression of emotion was culturally relative and determined, much like language. If emotional experiences and expressions were culturally specific, then the events or situations that produce the emotions must also be culturally specific. Subsequent strong evidence for the universal and biologically innate aspects of emotional expressions (Chapter 2) argued exactly the opposite: because emotion is a biologically innate phenomenon with a universal expressive component, there must be universality in the events and situations that provoke or produce emotional reactions. If emotion antecedents were not universal, it would be difficult to reconcile culturally specific antecedents with culturally universal experiences and expressions.

These arguments are of particular significance for our understanding of the emotions of the Japanese. Traditional Western European and American stereotypes of the Japanese would favor the culturally relative view of emotion antecedents, suggesting that events or situations that trigger emotions in Japan do not necessarily produce the same emotions elsewhere, and vice versa. It is true that people with experience interacting with Japanese people often find themselves in situations that would normally provoke in them an emotional reaction, but do not provoke the same reaction in the Japanese. For example, the rules governing the acceptance of jokes in social interaction and bantering are quite different in Japan compared with the United States; many Americans have found themselves laughing at their own jokes in the silence and stares of their Japanese colleagues. Alternatively, one may find oneself in a situation in which a Japanese person reacts in a way that may be totally different from what one would expect to be normal for an American in the same situation.

Certainly, the rules governing the display of emotional expression (discussed in Chapter 3) may be operative in these situations and will account for the cultural differences in the display of the emotional reactions. The question remains, then, whether the event provoked the same type of emotional response internally. That is, even if one observes a cultural difference in the emotional response on the outside, it is not clear whether the same emotion was elicited on the inside, and only the expression of the response was different. Alternatively, different emotions may have been aroused internally in the first place. The former would suggest cultural differences in display rules; the latter would suggest cultural differences in the antecedents and cognitive evaluations of the events and situations.

The question that concerns us here is that of the relationship between the display of emotion and emotional experience and internal processing, and possible cultural differences in that relationship. Previous research and writing on this topic have not generally questioned this relationship, most likely because there is an assumed correspondence between emotional expression and emotional experience. This assumption is rooted in American and Western psychology, which presumes that, in most situations, what one expresses is what one feels. Addressing possible cultural similarities and differences in antecedents and reactions within the knowledge of emotion display rules allows for the possibility of cultural differences in the relationship between emotions on the outside and on the inside.

Emotion Antecedents and Their Evaluations

Our research on emotion antecedents in Japan and their cognitive evaluations comes from the two studies described in Chapter 4 on the subjective, emotional experiences of the Japanese. In those studies (Matsumoto et al., 1988; Scherer et al., 1988), we compared the responses of a sample of Japanese respondents with comparable samples in Europe and the United States, who reported about events that had elicited anger, fear, happiness, sadness, disgust, guilt, and shame. Both studies were conducted as part of large cross-cultural surveys on the subjective experience of emotion that involved over 3,000 subjects in over 30 different countries (Scherer, Wallbott, & Summerfield, 1986; Wallbott & Scherer, 1986).

For each emotion, the respondents told us what sort of event or situation had brought about the emotion. Their open-ended responses were then coded by our laboratories into categories on the basis of the pattern of data obtained across all cultures in the sample, allowing for the use of the same set of codes across all responses and cultures. The cultural similarities and differences in these coded categories were tested, and are described more fully below. In addition, the respondents also provided us with data on the social context in which the events and emotions occurred. These open-ended responses were also coded by our research teams, and provided us with further data concerning the societal nature of the emotional experience in Japan. Finally, the respondents told us about how they evaluated—how and what they thought of—each of the events that produced the emotions they reported. More specifically, the respondents made a judgment on nine different categories concerning the event they reported. These categories were labeled Expectation, Pleasantness, Goal Facilitation, Event Fairness, Morality, Self-Esteem, Relationships, Responsibility, and Coping. These judgments provided the data by which we could examine how the Japanese cognitively processed the events and situations that produced the emotional reactions they reported.

Because this type of study had never been conducted with Japanese respondents, we were not at all sure what to expect from the data or the analyses. (One study on the same topic, however, published after ours by Mauro, Sato, and Tucker in 1992 reported generally the same results as our original research.) The findings we obtained suggested a number of ways in which the Japanese were at the same time similar to and different from Americans and Europeans both in the events that produced emotions and in their cognitive evaluation of those events. Below I present the major findings across both studies that are the most pertinent to the Japanese individual and culture. In a subsequent part of this chapter, I shall try to relate these findings to our previous discussions of Japanese culture, society, emotional expression, and display rules.

The Antecedents and Elicitors of Emotion in Japan

The codes for the emotion-eliciting events the Japanese respondents provided were collapsed into general categories (relationships with friends, achievement-related situations, etc.). Most categories were used for all emotions, but some were specific to only one emotion. We calculated standard inter-rater reliabilities on the coding, and found the coding categories to be quite reliable (about 0.80).

Because emotions are universal, we expected to find that events that were important in Europe for certain emotions would also be important in Japan and the United States. We also expected little difference in the rank order of antecedent events per emotion, because there were few differences among the European countries in previous analyses (see Scherer, Walbott, & Summerfield, 1986). However, the data showed the nature and pattern of antecedents to be quite different across the three cultures, with the major differences arising from the Japanese sample; the American and European samples were more similar to each other. In many cases, certain types of situations that are very important in Europe and the United States were not very frequent in Japan. Yet, some situations that frequently determine emotions in Japan are also important antecedents in Europe and the U.S.

I begin with the findings from the antecedent codes for four of the basic emotions—joy, anger, sadness, and fear—originally reported in Scherer et al. (1988).

ELICITORS OF JOY AND HAPPINESS

Cultural pleasures, birth of a new family member, and body-centered "basic pleasures" were more important antecedents for joy and happiness in the U.S. and Europe than they were in Japan. The relative insignificance of bodily pleasure seems to underline the stereotypical notion of the Japanese as a sober, hardworking and at times somewhat ascetic people. Also, the emphasis on self in relation to groups and others in Japan would seem to suggest that personal, individual experiences such as "bodily pleasures" would elicit relatively less positive emotion in Japan.

Other interesting cultural differences also existed. For example, personal achievement more often produced joy or happiness in the United States and Europe than it did in Japan. The fact that achievement, especially academic achievement, is in Japan a particularly stressful ritual probably explains the difference in response: Japanese youths most often attribute the cause of their academic efforts and achievements to family or other such groups rather than to personal, individual efforts or sacrifice. Also, because the individual Japanese tends to identify with groups instead of worrying about his or her individual self, personal achievement has less importance in Japan than does group or collective achievement. Although we did not assess respondents' reactions to group-affiliated achievement situations, I suspect that these kinds of events would produce more happiness and joy in Japan than in the United States or Europe.

There were some cultural similarities in the antecedent events to joy and happiness. For example, relationships produced as much joy and happiness in Japan as they did in Europe and the United States, and so, too, did temporary meetings of friends. These data are to be expected, since interpersonal relationships with ingroup members are a major part of a Japanese person's physical and psychological life and consciousness, and would naturally form the basis for many different emotional reactions.

ELICITORS OF SADNESS AND GRIEF

We found cultural differences in almost every class of elicitor of sadness and grief, among them, most strikingly, the response to the death of a family member or close friend. Whereas both in Europe and in the United States such events accounted for about one-fifth of all sad experiences, only one-twentieth of sad situations in Japan were due to death. We interpreted this finding as related to Japanese cultural beliefs about death, particularly concerning the rules of veneration for ancestors, and the cultural rituals that exist that allow friends and family members who pass on to remain a vital spiritual part of the family. These rituals have their roots in Japanese Shinto and Buddhist religions, and play a major, though often silent, role in Japanese culture. Western cultures do not share these attitudes about death, and see death as more of a permanent separation rather than the continuation of the relationship on a spiritual level.

Sadness due to problems in relationships was very common in Japan. This finding, too, is related to the importance of interpersonal relationships in Japanese culture, and the psychological meaning attached to such relationships. Problems in relationships have substantially more detrimental meaning to Japanese people than they do to non-Japanese, thereby accounting for greater amounts of sadness in relation to such problems. On the other hand, the Japanese were relatively less saddened by both temporary and permanent separation, especially in comparison with Americans. One possible explanation of this finding is that, perhaps because of geographical distances, separations from persons with whom one is involved in a close relationship are more frequent in the United States, less frequent in Europe, and even less frequent in Japan. In addition to the more restricted geographic mobility in Japan (and some parts of Europe), there is a difference in the closeness and permanence of relationships. In the United States, the ending of old relationships and the formation of new ones are rather frequent phenomena. The greater permanence of relationships in Japan would explain why sadness would tend to be based on events that happen within a relationship rather than on separations.

Another difference in sadness elicitation was found for the impact of world news. The Japanese were rarely saddened by world events, whereas the Europeans, and even more so the Americans, were very saddened by these events. The difference seems unrelated to a differential incidence of world news relevant for the different samples, although it may have been the case at the time of data collection (mid-1980s) that world events were more salient for the Americans than for the Japanese. Rather, this finding probably reflects the reliance in Japanese culture on immediate personal relationships with "ingroup" members, and the distancing of empathy and emotion with persons or events outside one's primary group. Because things that occur in the "world" would not necessarily have immediate, personal impact on one's relationships with ingroup others, such events would be much less likely to produce sadness. Americans and Europeans, who make far fewer distinctions between ingroup and outgroup others, would be more likely to feel emotion at disturbing world news, however little it affected one in a personal way.

ELICITORS OF FEAR AND ANXIETY

The largest cultural differences in the antecedent situations for fear arose in three categories: fear of strangers, risky situations, and relationships. For Americans, fear of strangers was the most frequent category, followed by fear of failure in achievement situations. For the Europeans, fear of strangers and fear of traffic situations were the most frequent fear-producing events. For the Japanese, fear of novel situations, fear of failure in achievement situations, and fear of traffic were the most frequent categories; fear of strangers was almost insignificant. These findings were most likely related to the differential incidence of threatening events in the three groups, especially related to crime. The perception of crime is much higher in the United States than it is in Japan, where it is not uncommon for young adults, teenagers, women, and girls to walk around on the streets at night, returning home or in transit between places. This is unheard of in many areas of the United States, particularly in the larger urban areas.

One category for which there was a much higher incidence for the Japanese respondents was relationship-produced fear—in situations that might involve hurting one's parents, or angering one's boyfriend or girlfriend. This finding probably reflects the Japanese culture's constant monitoring and regulation of social relationships, particularly in relation to social transgressions, and is congruent with other findings reported earlier concerning the importance of relationships.

ELICITORS OF ANGER AND RAGE

For this category, the Japanese respondents were again radically different from the Europeans or Americans. The Japanese reported much more anger toward strangers than did the Americans or Europeans, but much less anger in relationships with known others. In a collective culture like Japan's, it is easy to experience anger toward members of outgroups—people outside one's inner circle; in fact, expressing anger toward strangers and other outgroup members serves an important function because it solidifies one's role and place within one's ingroup. People in collective cultures such as Japan's need to make greater differentiations between ingroups and outgroups, because the entire culture and society revolve around group membership. At the same time, the Japanese need to minimize anger toward ingroup members, to maintain group harmony and cohesion.

Another major difference was with situations of injustice. These provoked anger very frequently in the United States and Europe, but very infrequently in Japan. One explanation of the difference could be that in Japan the rules of justice are more strictly applied in behavior; another explanation could be that cultural display rules dictate the suppression of anger, which leads to an acceptance of injustices in order to avoid confrontation. This would be especially true if the injustice was inflicted on outgroup others. In anger-provoking situations involving matters of achievement and inconvenience, there seemed to be no cultural differences, the Japanese reporting as many incidences of these types of events as the Americans and Europeans.

In sum, although many of the emotion elicitors in Japan gave rise to the same emotions in the U.S. and Europe, there were a number of differences in the *relative importance* of the various events for the Japanese. Events that call forth a certain emotion by an American may not necessarily bring forth the same emotion for a Japanese person. Likewise, an event that produces an emotion for a Japanese person may not necessarily produce the same emotional reaction for the American.

Misunderstandings and miscommunication can easily occur because of these differences. If one expects a certain emotional reaction from a Japanese person and it is not forthcoming, it is easy to believe that the Japanese person is either emotionless or strange. You may think the same thing if you witness an emotion that you think is inappropriate. Japanese people can, and do, have the same misperceptions of Americans and other non-Japanese. These differences can be at least partially resolved by recognizing first that emotion elicitors can be different across cultures. Thus, not only is the display of an emotion likely to be different in Japan because of cultural display rules that are governed by social circumstances; there are likely to be cultural differences in the antecedents that bring about emotions, and what kinds of emotions are elicited in the first place.

The Ecology of Emotion-Eliciting Events

It was important in our research to understand the circumstances of emotion-producing events. We asked the Japanese subjects to tell us where they were and who else was present when they had their emotional experiences. We coded their responses according to whether the situation occurred inside or outside familiar or unfamiliar settings; whether they occurred when alone, with another, or with a group of others; and whether the others that were present were familiar or not. We expected, of course, that the ecology of the Japanese emotional experience would be different from that of Americans and Europeans.

SETTINGS

We found a number of cultural differences in the settings in which emotions occurred. For example, joy occurred very rarely inside unfamiliar places in Japan (about 5 percent) compared with the United States and Europe (about 20 percent each). The Japanese were more likely to experience sadness inside unfamiliar settings and outside, whereas the Americans and Europeans were much less likely to. These differences speak to the nature of cultural influences on emotions in different social settings. The Japanese need to display reserve in their expressions of joy and positive emotions in unfamiliar places, in order to maintain social distinctions among settings and situations. The Japanese are also more likely to suppress feelings of sadness in familiar settings, reserving these for unfamiliar situations.

For fear, the Japanese reported significantly fewer fear-producing incidences inside familiar places than did the Americans or Europeans. At the same time, the Japanese reported more fear outside and in unfamiliar places. These differences speak to the cultural differences in the safety and intimacy attributed by Japanese to familiar settings, because of their ingroup nature.

Finally, for anger, the Japanese reported significantly fewer anger-producing events inside familiar places, and more anger-producing events outside than did the Americans. Again, this pattern of data is consistent with the ingroup-outgroup distinction, since Japanese will be more likely to have socially disruptive emotions such as anger elicited and expressed outside the ingroup circle.

INTERACTANTS

Most emotions occurred when respondents were alone, in a dyad, or in a small group, and there were important cultural differences in the relative frequencies of each of these three categories. Across the board, the Japanese experienced more emotions in dyads than did the Americans and Europeans, and they experienced significantly fewer emotions alone than did the respondents from the other two cultures. At the same time, respondents in all three cultures reported that about three-fourths of all situations producing anger, sadness, and joy involved familiar people. Even within these data, the Japanese tended to report a significantly greater percentage of events involving familiar people than did the Americans or Europeans. For fear, the Japanese reported that a majority of fear-producing situations involved familiar people; a majority of the Americans and Europeans, however, reported that fear was elicited with unfamiliar people.

These data especially speak to the importance of the social meanings and roles of emotions in Japan. In the United States, Americans typically view emotions as important mainly because they have individual, personal meaning to oneself. For the Japanese, emotions have more social relevance, helping to maintain (or break) interpersonal bonds and social relationships. Given cultural differences in the influence of society and culture in the U.S. and Japan, it is no wonder that the Japanese would report relatively fewer emotions when alone, and relatively more in dyads, than would the Americans or Europeans.

In addition to the question of social meaning of emotions, a further puzzle is that of the true frequency of occurrence of the three social situations across the cultures compared. That is, if the Japanese, Americans, and Europeans do indeed spend different amounts of time in each of these social categories, the differences in the frequency of emotions may simply be a consequence of opportunity or lack thereof; because we had no data on this point, there is no way to judge. On some levels, however, the possibility of confounding is inevitable because of the intimate nature of the relationship between such frequency of occurrence and the social meaning of emotion: each might contribute to the other reciprocally, in which case separating the confound becomes only academically meaningful while bordering on the socially and practically irrelevant.

Cognitive Evaluations of Emotion-Eliciting Events in Japan

A final way by which we tried to examine cultural similarities and differences in emotional experience was to ask the respondents to evaluate the events that produced their emotional reactions. For each emotional experience they told us about, the respondents rated each of the following (in the order given): (1) how much they *expected* the situation to occur; (2) how *pleasant* the event was; (3) whether the event *helped or hindered* goals or needs; (4) whether the situation was *fair or unfair;* (5) who was *responsible* for the situation; (6) possible *actions* as a result of the event; (7) *morality* of the event; (8) effects on *self-esteem or self-confidence*; (9) effects on relationships. The respondents' answers to these questions provided us with important clues to the ways in which they cognitively evaluated the events. We tested for American vs. Japanese cultural differences in the responses, and formed yet another interesting picture of how the Japanese were at the same time the same as and different from the Americans.

CULTURAL SIMILARITIES IN EVALUATIONS

The Japanese did not differ from the Americans in their expectation of the events, the intrinsic pleasantness of the event, the facilitation or hindrance of goals, the degree to which they thought the event or situation was fair or moral, and the effects of the situation on their relationships with others. These similarities are interesting because they suggest some degree of culture-constant, and perhaps universal, ways of evaluating or appraising emotion-eliciting events. These appraisal mechanisms resemble similar appraisal and evaluative processes postulated by other students of emotion, most notably Lazarus (1966, 1991), and more recently Leventhal (1984) and Scherer (1984). These authors suggest that an appraisal process is responsible for evaluating characteristics of possible emotion-eliciting stimuli, and for informing a primary response to the stimulus in terms of an emotion. That these cognitive dimensions in our studies produced no differences between the cultures, while at the same time being discriminative of the seven different emotions included in the study, suggests the possible universality of these appraisal processes (for a fuller discussion of these issues, see Matsumoto, et al., 1988).

CULTURAL DIFFERENCES IN COGNITIVE EVALUATIONS

Still, there were some notable cultural differences in the cognitive evaluations of the emotion elicitors, not only related to our previous discussion of Japanese culture but also interesting for their possible bearing on secondary emotional reactions. For example, emotions generally had negative effects on the Japanese self-esteem, whereas this was definitely not the case for the Americans. One possible explanation of this finding is related to the notion that emotion regulation and control in Japan is viewed as a more mature, socialized trait and skill. If the Japanese people allow emotions to run their course, they may view themselves as less in control of themselves, and therefore report more negative effects on their self-esteem.

There were also cultural differences in how the Japanese assigned responsibility for their emotions and the events that produced them. Americans most often attributed their sadness-producing events to other people; the Japanese respondents were more willing to attribute the causes of their sadness to themselves rather than to others. Again, this finding points to how the Japanese way of thinking is doubly burdensome on the individual by attributing the cause of this negative emotion to themselves. One possible explanation of this is that the attribution of the cause of sadness to oneself rather than to others may act to maintain harmony with others, rather than instigating possible disharmony and disruption with the attribution to others. In American society, it is easier to attribute the responsibility for one's emotions, especially negative ones, to others; the lack of a strong emphasis on interpersonal harmony implies a corresponding lack of concern for blaming others for one's negative emotions.

Americans also tended to attribute the cause of joy, fear, and shame to other people. The Japanese attributed the cause of these emotions to chance or fate. These findings also suggest the importance of maintaining harmonious relationships with others by avoiding potential conflict that would arise from attributions of causality for one's emotions. There were cultural differences between the Americans and Japanese in the degree to which they were willing to attribute responsibility for their emotions. For all emotions studied, the Japanese made fewer attributions of any type than the Americans, again suggesting the importance of avoiding potential conflict through such attributions.

The avoidance of attributing causality for one's emotions to other people perhaps has contributed to views of Japanese people as being totally unconcerned with emotion. I disagree with this stereotype. A more likely reason has to do with the real power of emotion, and its possible effects on social relations. The Japanese realize that emotion must be controlled in a certain way in order for their culture to survive; thus, the Japanese culture fosters the avoidance of such direct confrontation, whether it be related to attribution of emotion causality, or any other type of direct statement that may harm one's re-

lationships with others. Because other cultures rely less on interpersonal harmony, there is less need to avoid direct attributions. The
attribution of causality of one's emotions to others is not perceived as
a strong threat to interpersonal relationships, and there is less need
or pressure to maintain harmony in such relationships.

Finally, we asked the respondents in our studies to identify the
behavior or action that was most appropriate as a result of their emotional experience. Only one cultural difference was found, but this
was found consistently across most of the emotions: more Japanese
than Americans believed that no action was necessary as a result of
their emotional experience. This finding is directly related to the findings concerning attributions of responsibility. If the Japanese respondents are less willing to make direct attributions of causality for
their emotions, it follows that there is less need for any action to occur afterward. This reasoning is congruent with my suggestion that
this pattern of thinking and behavior results from the Japanese cultural emphasis on maintaining interpersonal harmony, and how this
harmony is protected by suppressing actions that could be elicited by
emotional experiences.

*Understanding Cultural Similarities
and Differences in Emotion Antecedents:
A Model of Antecedent Meaning*

The cultural differences that we observed between the Japanese,
American, and European respondents were, on the whole, matters of
degree rather than of total disagreement. That is, it was not that news
or achievement situations produced emotions for one culture but not
for another, rather, these, and other, elicitors produced different degrees of the various emotions in the three cultures.

In understanding cultural differences in emotion antecedents, it
is important to use a concept integral to the understanding of antecedent events themselves—manifest vs. latent content. *Manifest content* refers to the actual "facts" relating to an event. The manifest
content of passing an exam, for example, would be the actual test
score one obtained, and the evaluation by the teacher that one had
received a passing grade. The manifest content of a death event would
be the actual fact of the death.

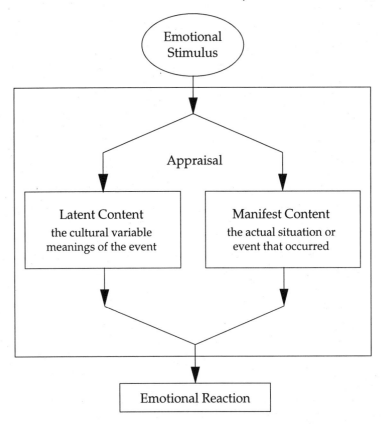

Fig. 4. The Processing of Manifest and Latent Content in the Appraisal of an Emotion Antecedent

Latent content refers to the underlying meaning of an event or situation. This meaning typically refers to the relationship of the event to one's sense or definition of self; latent contents are by definition culturally variable, because one's definition of self, and the ways in which one interprets events and derives meanings from them, are all bound by culture.

In eliciting an emotion, both manifest and latent contents must be interpreted, such as in the process diagrammed in Figure 4. Latent content, being a subjective quality, may vary enormously depending on the people involved and their personal and cultural backgrounds. For example, passing an exam may be interpreted by one person as a totally personal testament to his or her own self-achievement and efforts. Another person, from his point of view, may interpret the same event (i.e., an event with the same manifest content) as a personal achievement, but also as a marker of his obligations to those who aided him in the achievement, and as a signal of further such social obligations.

Differences in latent content underlie American vs. Japanese interpretations of the events and situations that produce their emotions. The American culture fosters a construction of the sense of self that centers around oneself as a unique individual. The Japanese culture fosters a definition of self that is intertwined with group and society. Events with the same manifest content (e.g., academic achievement) can produce differences in emotional reaction because of the differences in the latent content associated with the event, which is culturally determined and variable. This would be congruent with the data presented earlier in this chapter and reported in our research that academic achievement situations produce greater joy in Americans than in Japanese. Again, this is not to say that achievement situations produce no joy in our Japanese respondents. Rather, cultural differences in the latent content of the various events and situations aid in the production of general, cultural differences in the different types of emotional reactions reported by our respondents.

In another example, when death is the manifest content, the latent content can be culturally variable in the same way. In the American culture, death can be construed as a personal loss to oneself. In the Japanese culture, death is certainly construed in this way too, but it is also interpreted as the achievement of another state of being; and the loss is minimized by cultural and social institutions that revere the dead and place them in the home near oneself. These types of cultural differences in latent content may contribute to cultural differences in the degree to which the same event (i.e., death) will produce the same emotion (i.e., sadness) in the two cultures.

The concept of manifest vs. latent content of emotion antecedent events is a powerful one that would allow for the integration and complementation of two disparate views of emotion elicitation. Early in this chapter, I described two schools of thought concerning emotion elicitors. One suggests that emotion elicitors had to be culturally relative, because emotions and their expressions were culturally rela-

tive. Cultural differences in the manifest content of the emotion antecedents reported in our research certainly suggest this view. The
other school suggested that emotion elicitors were culturally universal; that is, because emotions and their expressions were biologically
innate and evolutionarily adaptive, the situations and events that produced them must also be universal.

Differences between these two points of view can be integrated
into a single conceptual framework concerning emotion antecedents
via the incorporation of the concept of manifest and latent content in
antecedent situations. Cultures will vary, sometimes greatly, in the
manifest content of the antecedent situations and events that produce
emotions. But I suggest that cultures are quite similar in the latent
content underlying the events and situations that produce similar
emotions. The data presented in this chapter are only speculative and
require further empirical and theoretical work; still, if we can extract
the latent definitions and meanings of the various antecedent events,
especially so far as they relate to the impact of the event on one's sense
of self and the relationship between self and others, I predict that
there will be a considerable degree of overlap across cultures, Japan
included, in the antecedents and elicitors of emotion. On the surface,
however, cultural differences in the manifest content of situations
and events will remain.

Understanding Cultural Similarities and Differences in the Cognitive Evaluations of Emotions: A Model of the Appraisal Process

There are also considerable cultural similarities and differences
in the cognitive evaluations of the emotion antecedents. I believe that
these patterns of data arise from the nature of the evaluation process
that occurs when an emotion is elicited. An antecedent event (both
manifest and latent content) will be appraised first along several dimensions that inform the individual about the nature of the stimulus
and its relationship to the self. The data from our studies suggest that
a number of these dimensions may be universal and culturally in-
variant, such as expectation, intrinsic pleasantness, and so on. An
emotional reaction is thus formed on the basis of these evaluations
(see Figure 5).

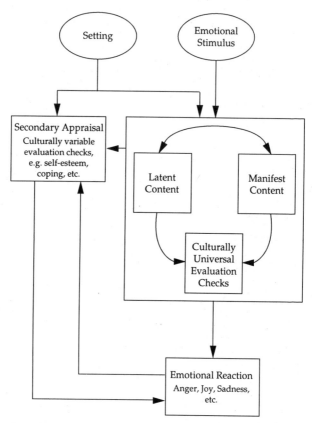

Fig. 5. The Influence of Content, Setting, and Primary and Secondary Appraisal on the Elicitation of Emotion

After one has formed an emotional reaction, the next step is a second appraisal process, which, unlike the perhaps automatic or subconscious first appraisal, is more deliberate and involves a more rational, thinking process. In this second appraisal, one integrates information from the first (primary) appraisal, the emotional reaction, the nature or ecology of the situation, and the latent content of the emotional antecedent. In this secondary appraisal, the interpretation of all these aspects of the entire experience is naturally more culturally variable than the initial emotional appraisal, because the information that is brought into appraisal at this time is more socially relevant (the interactants, the latent content of the elicitor, the appropriateness of the response, etc.). Cultural differences will be observed in this second appraisal process and its effects.

This type of appraisal model would explain why we obtained both cultural similarities and differences in our data on evaluations. In the case of cultural similarities, the dimensions respondents rated may have been related to the initial appraisal process, thereby being more "basic" to the elicitation of emotion and panculturally universal. The second appraisal process, however, brought together socially and culturally relevant, learned information, which produced cultural differences. This information includes cultural differences in the latent content and in the ecology of the event. It is not surprising, therefore, that this process would produce cultural differences in the evaluation process here, including cultural differences in self-esteem, responsibility, and coping behaviors. Emotions for the Japanese should produce differential effects on self-esteem, attributions of responsibility, and coping behaviors, which is what we found.

The Role of the Ecology of the Emotions

The impact of the ecology of the emotion event (i.e., the setting, the interactants, etc.) is extremely important in the production of cultural differences in emotion elicitation. The ecology of the event contributes to the emotion process in a number of ways. First, it affects the latent content of an emotion antecedent. That is, the meaning derived from an emotion elicitor must be dependent upon the context in which the elicitor occurs.

Second, the ecology of emotion affects the secondary appraisal process described above. Context, including situation and interactants, plays a large role when individuals reevaluate the event and their initial reactions, especially in relation to attributions of responsibility and coping behaviors. Differences in either the physical or social context may dramatically alter the responses and appraisal processes that occur at this point.

Third, the ecology of the emotional experience must have an important impact on the nature of display rules governing the expression of one's emotion. It is these contextual cues that will govern the modification, if any, of one's emotional displays, depending on the social circumstance.

The ecology of emotion is one of the most crucial aspects of emotion elicitation and appraisal processes for the Japanese. Context and setting should have much larger effects for the Japanese than for Americans, especially in relation to self-other relationships. Because the Japanese must continuously monitor the impact of their emotions and reactions to self-other relationships and group process, the relative contribution of context is much larger in Japan than in the United States. The same event occurring in two different contexts (e.g., when with one's family vs. when with one's work colleagues) will elicit different emotional responses and appraisal processes in Japan. By contrast, in the American culture, which places greater emphasis on the self than on context or setting, there is much more concern for self-consistency in response across contexts and situations. This consistency results in less variation in emotion response across situations for Americans.

Conclusions

In this chapter, we have seen how the antecedents of emotion in Japan, and their cognitive evaluations, are similar to and different from those of the United States and Europe. Although the elicitors and appraisal processes of emotion do not readily come to mind when thinking about emotions, the data and interpretations so far presented show how are important these are in the emotion process and how important they are to our understanding of cultural similarities and differences in emotion between the Japanese and other cultures. Many of these findings and interpretations warrant further research into the nature of antecedents and evaluations. Of particular interest in years to come will be attempts to extract latent content in antecedent events, and tests of similarities and differences on this latent content. Also of particular interest should be the extrapolation of primary and secondary appraisal processes, and the incorporation of secondary emotional reactions to the model. As I have mentioned in other chapters, I believe that secondary emotional reactions are extremely important to understanding the emotional lives of the Japanese. Research on this important topic needs to elucidate on the nature and function of these secondary reactions.

Chapter 6

Judgments of Emotion in Japan

Another important but often neglected aspect of human emotion is *emotional perception*—that is, how we see and judge others and their emotions. Some people seem to have a knack for this kind of social perception; others find judgment difficult. And even if two people observing the same behavior make the same judgment about what emotion is being expressed, they may have different opinions about the degree of emotion, or its actual intensity. Emotional perception is important to the system of emotion in that the way in which we perceive others directly influences our own emotional experiences and emotional expressions. Our judgments of emotion color our own experiences, and our experiences, in turn, color our judgments. Thus, our emotional perceptions are not just judgments of events and behaviors external to us with no personal meaning; they have direct and substantial meaning to how we experience our own lives.

Chapter 3 discusses cultural display rules (Ekman & Friesen, 1969), which govern the display or expression of emotion depending on social circumstance. Chapter 4 discussed "feeling rules," the culturally and socially prescribed guidelines that govern our subjective experience of emotion. This chapter describes how culture and society also have rules governing emotional perception. Buck (1984) has coined the term "decoding rules" to refer to these culturally and socially prescribed rules of emotional perception. This chapter will present the findings from a number of cross-cultural studies that have examined how the Japanese perceive other people's emotions. The Japanese are similar to, but at the same time different from, people of other cultures in their recognition of universal facial expressions of emotion. The Japanese also differ from non-Japanese in their judgments of how strongly others are expressing emotion. This chapter also examines how the Japanese judge smiles, the expression most used to mask or conceal their true emotions.

Japanese Perceptions of Emotion

Stereotypical notions about the Japanese would suggest that the Japanese do not perceive the same emotions as non-Japanese, or in the same ways. One could reason, for example, that because the Japanese have learned to express emotions so differently from non-Japanese, they also learn to perceive them differently. That is, if the Japanese learn to smile every time they are angry at a boss, then others observing them will come to believe that when they smile, they are not necessarily happy. In fact, they may be angry. In short, this notion suggests that the existence of cultural display rules produces learned expectancies about emotion when judging others, because one expects that the expressions of others are occurring within the context of the display rules that are appropriate for their own culture.

Until the 1960s, this was the predominant view of Japanese emotional perception. It was supported by anthropological works expounding Japanese and Western cultural differences, and by social psychological research testing for cultural differences in emotional perception. The few studies that were conducted before the 1960s did seem to support the culture-specific view of emotional expression, and thus perception, suggesting that the Japanese learned to interpret emotions differently from people of other cultures (Chapter 2). Research establishing the universality of emotional expression added a new dimension to this argument. Because emotional expressions are universal, it became theoretically possible that the Japanese were in some ways similar to people of other cultures in their judgments of emotion. If that proved to be true, then the question to be studied became in what ways were the perceptions of the Japanese similar to, and in what ways different from, the perceptions of people of other cultures.

Fortunately, there is an abundance of research that answers this question. The original universality research conducted by Ekman and Izard, for example, included samples from Japan in judgment or perception studies (Ekman, 1972; Izard, 1971). In the mid-1980s, data on the judgments of emotion from Japan were included in yet another large-scale, cross-cultural study of emotion judgments, this time involving data from ten different cultures (Ekman et al., 1987). Since then, our laboratory has conducted two more judgment studies in Japan (Matsumoto, 1992a; Matsumoto & Ekman, 1989), further adding to our already large database on Japanese judgments of emotion.

The methodology involved in most of these studies was similar and relatively straightforward. Observers in all cultures were shown a series of facial expressions of emotion. In some studies, the facial expressions included only universal expressions such as those depicted in Chapter 2; in other studies, they included universal emotions and nonemotional faces. In some studies, observers made a categorical judgment of which emotion was being portrayed in the face by selecting a single emotion term from a list of alternatives that they felt best described the emotion portrayed. In other studies, the observers made multiple-scale ratings of intensity on each of a number of emotion terms. In yet other studies the observers made a single rating of intensity with no emotion labels. In studies described elsewhere (e.g., see Ekman, 1994), observers made open-ended judgments.

Thus, the data on Japanese judgments of emotion have spanned different methodologies in various studies with multiple research paradigms, and are not artifacts of a single paradigm. In spite of differences in the methodologies, however, the findings have been quite consistent. In general, these findings point specifically to ways in which the Japanese are indeed similar to, and at the same time different from, Westerners and people of other cultures in their judgments of facial expressions of emotion.

Cultural Similarities in the Recognition of Facial Expressions of Emotion in Japan

As discussed in Chapter 2, studies conducted over twenty years ago (Ekman, 1972, 1973; Ekman & Friesen, 1971; Ekman, Sorenson &

Friesen, 1969; Izard, 1971) and replicated in many studies since (see Matsumoto, Wallbott, & Scherer, 1989) have shown that the recognition of facial expressions of emotion is universal. In one early study (Ekman, 1972), for example, Japanese respondents were shown photographs of the universal emotions, and were asked to judge what emotion, if any, the people in the photographs were displaying. Their judgments were compared with the judgments of people from the United States, Argentina, Chile, and Brazil. The judgments of the Japanese did not differ at all from the judgments of the respondents in the other cultures. When the Americans saw joy, the Japanese also saw joy; when the people from South America saw anger and disgust, the Japanese also saw anger and disgust.

In another set of studies, respondents from Japan and other cultures were given the chance to describe not only which emotion they saw, but other emotions, if any, in addition to the first emotion (Ekman et al., 1987). Again, the Japanese were consistent with people of other cultures in their primary judgments of emotion. That is, the emotion scale given the highest mean intensity rating across all scales was the same for the Japanese as it was for people of the other countries surveyed. Moreover, there was consistency across the cultures in the secondary emotional message. For example, when viewing a photograph depicting anger, all the cultures agreed that the emotion portrayed was anger, with some disgust and contempt.

In this study, in addition to consistency in the primary emotion scale, there were also cultural similarities in the secondary emotional message, which was defined to be the emotion scale given the second highest mean rating within a culture. The Japanese were consistent with observers in other cultures, for instance, in their perceptions of fear expressions. When they saw fear, they often reported that they saw not only fear but also the secondary emotion of surprise. Respondents in other cultures saw these two emotions, in this order, as well.

Two other studies point to other ways in which the Japanese are similar in their recognition of emotion to people of other cultures (Ekman et al., 1987; Matsumoto & Ekman, 1989). In these studies, respondents were given the chance to report that they saw no emotion at all. (Almost all the research conducted until this time forced the respondents to make a choice of emotion. Critics of this approach suggested that cultural similarities were often found because respondents chose response alternatives that really were the lesser of several evils—that they really didn't see any emotion, but since they had to choose, they chose one.) Again, even when the subjects were given response alternatives that allowed for a "No Choice" option, the Japanese were in complete agreement concerning which emotion was being portrayed in all the stimuli that we used.

Finally, we examined whether the Japanese differed in their perceptions of relative intensity among emotional expressions. For example, when presented with two different emotional expressions, one portrayed intensely and the other less intensely, would the Japanese be in agreement with people from other cultures that the one portrayed more intensely was indeed more intense? This is an interesting question, because we might expect the Japanese to infer more emotional intensity into weak expressions because they guess that the person is actually experiencing more emotion than he or she is showing. The findings were clear: across all comparisons made, the Japanese were again in complete agreement with respondents from other cultures concerning which expression was more intense.

The findings from these studies provide quite conclusive evidence that the ability to recognize emotions is universal. The Japanese will recognize the same emotions in each of the faces presented in Chapter 2 as well as people of other cultures. These conclusions were obtained despite differences in the stimuli, the instructions provided to the respondents, and the response alternatives used in making judgments. Different researchers in different countries, in different laboratories, using different procedures, have arrived at the same conclusions.

Although the exact mechanism underlying universal emotion judgment and recognition is not clear, I believe it is related to the existence of the Facial Affect Program, described in Chapter 2, which stores the prototypical facial configurations of the universal emotions. This program is considered to be biologically innate, inherent to all people regardless of culture, race, or gender. Because of the existence of this program, emotion recognition can occur through a process similar to template matching, where incoming stimuli are compared against the facial prototype of emotion, and judgments occur based on the matching comparison.

Cultural Differences in Japanese Recognition Accuracy of Universal Facial Expressions of Emotion

Even though the Japanese have the same ability to recognize emotions in others as do people from other cultures, another question arises concerning whether they exercise the ability to the same degree as others do. The ability to recognize universal facial expressions of emotion does not necessarily mean that people in different cultures all use this ability to the same degree. Some cultures may suppress this ability, while some cultures may encourage it. Which of these two alternatives may be occurring for the Japanese is not entirely clear. On the one hand, one might expect the Japanese, who need to suppress or hide their emotions in many different social situations, to have a keen sense of recognizing emotions. This line of reasoning suggests that the ability to recognize emotions accurately is inversely related to the expression of emotion—that is, as the Japanese learn more and more to suppress, conceal, or alter their emotional expressions, they become better at recognizing emotions in others from the slightest expressive cues. On the other hand, the same cultural rules may suggest that Japanese are worse than others in recognizing emotions. That is, because the Japanese have learned to modify or suppress their expressions of emotion, they have also learned to suppress their perceptions of emotions in others.

In order to examine whether or not the Japanese are any better or worse than non-Japanese in recognizing the universal emotions, we first reexamined the data originally collected by Ekman and Izard some seventeen years earlier. We found that, although the Japanese did not differ in recognition accuracy rates for emotions such as happiness and surprise, they did differ from the non-Japanese samples in their perceptions of fear, anger, disgust, and contempt. In these cases, the Japanese actually did worse than the non-Japanese, suggesting that the Japanese culture acts to suppress the recognition of these emotions.

In another study (Matsumoto, 1989a), we examined whether cultural differences in recognition accuracy were systematically related to differences in the degree to which the cultures were group or status oriented. Again, we correlated the judgment data collected by Ekman and Izard with cultural dimension scores derived independently via

Hofstede's (1980, 1983) work on cultural values in the workplace. As predicted, the degree of recognition accuracy was indeed related to the type of culture; collective cultures such as that of Japan tended to do worse at recognizing emotions. Cultures that were highly status differentiating, again like the Japanese, also tended to do worse than cultures that were low status differentiating.

One major limitation to this research has been the nature of the stimuli used in the various studies. Almost without exception, all the stimuli have portrayed Caucasian posers, with unequal numbers of males and females and poser redundancy. These characteristics violate several methodological requirements necessary for adequate tests of cultural differences, thus rendering previous findings concerning cultural differences in emotional perception questionable. In the mid-1980s, our laboratory (Matsumoto, 1986; Matsumoto & Ekman, 1988) undertook the task of producing a new set of stimuli that addressed these concerns.

Our efforts resulted in a set of photographs we called the Japanese and Caucasian Facial Expressions of Emotion (JACFEE). The JACFEE consists of photographs of 56 different people—28 Caucasian and 28 Japanese posers. There are eight photos for each of seven universal emotions (anger, contempt, disgust, fear, happiness, sadness, and surprise), with four photos each (two males and two females) of Caucasians and Japanese. All photos have been coded using a facial measurement technique known as the Facial Action Coding System (FACS—Ekman & Friesen, 1978). We have used the JACFEE reliably in a number of studies involving judgments from different countries and cultures, all agreeing in the emotional content of the photos. The expressions depicted in Chapter 2 come from the JACFEE.

In one of these studies (Matsumoto, 1991), we examined the Japanese recognition accuracy rates of the universal facial expressions of emotion. Japanese and American respondents were shown the JACFEE and were asked to judge which emotion was being portrayed in each of the photographs. Again, there was no difference between the American and Japanese judgments of happy and surprise photos; the Japanese were worse than the Americans, however, in judging anger, disgust, fear, and sadness. Moreover, this finding was obtained regardless of the race or gender of the poser.

The findings from all the studies have provided quite solid evidence that the Japanese have lower recognition accuracy rates for the negative universal emotions of anger, disgust, fear, and sadness. It appears that, although the ability to recognize emotions is universal, the Japanese culture works to hinder the correct perception of some of these emotions. Earlier, we discussed how the expression of these emotions can be detrimental to social relationships and interpersonal harmony, thus requiring that the culture sanction their expression through cultural display rules. We suspect that the Japanese culture works similarly to suppress the perception of these emotions.

Such a cultural suppression makes intuitive sense. The suppression of the displays of these emotions is really only part of the Japanese culture's influence on emotion; if the emergence of these emotions is detrimental to the Japanese culture, then the perception of these same emotions must also be suppressed. If not, then these emotions will exist, at least in the eyes of the perceiver, thus leading to detrimental effects to interpersonal harmony. If they are not perceived, then they in effect do not exist, thus protecting the interpersonal relationships within which these emotions are perceived.

Cultural Differences in Japanese Judgments of the Intensity of Other's Emotional Expressions

In the ten-culture study of Ekman et al. (1987) described above, respondents judged not only which emotion they perceived in the stimuli but also how intensely they perceived it. It was reasoned that, if the perception of facial expressions of emotion was indeed universal, the respondents in the different cultures would agree on the level of intensity they thought was depicted in the stimuli. However, the data indicated that there were cultural differences in the intensity levels: post hoc analyses indicated that the Asian cultures (Japan and Hong Kong) attributed lower intensities to the expressions than did the Caucasian cultures. This analysis was relevant because the stimuli used in this study included only Caucasian posers; thus, the respondents in the non-Caucasian cultures could easily tell that the posers were not of their own culture, and adjust their ratings according to this knowledge. The respondents in the Asian cultures hesitated in giving high intensity ratings to the faces either because of politeness or because of ignorance concerning the cultural display rules of the Caucasian posers.

In another post hoc analysis, we compared the intensity ratings of the English-speaking countries against those of non-English-speaking countries. This comparison was important because the cultural differences originally found may have been attributable to differences in the intensities of the emotion lexicons of the cultures in the study. Indeed, we found that the English-speaking countries (the United States and Scotland) attributed greater intensity to the universal facial expressions than did the non-English-speaking countries. These data suggested that the intensity level of the English words used in the response scales may have been different from that of the translations of those words used in the other cultures. Respondents would make their rating not only on the basis of the intensity they perceived in the stimuli but also on the basis of the words they used to make their ratings. Cultural differences in the ratings might therefore have reflected differences in the words just as much as differences in the expressions.

In order to retest the findings about cultural differences in judgments of intensity and to uncover the bases underlying these differences, we conducted another study in which we compared the intensity judgments of Americans and Japanese using the JACFEE (Matsumoto & Ekman, 1989). We reasoned that if the Japanese adjusted their intensity ratings according to the race of the poser, they would rate the Japanese photos differently from the Caucasian photos.

The data indicated that the Japanese did indeed give lower intensity ratings to the expressions than the Americans, thus replicating the earlier findings. But the Japanese attributed lower ratings to the expressions regardless of whether the expression was posed by a Caucasian or by a Japanese person, and regardless of whether the poser was male or female. Thus, poser race had nothing to do with the cultural differences in judgment.

In another condition of the same study, respondents made the same type of intensity judgments using an anchorless rating scale that used no emotion words in English or in Japanese. We included this condition in order to eliminate the possible effects of differences between the English and Japanese emotion lexicons. The data analysis produced the same results as earlier: the Japanese gave lower intensity ratings than the Americans to the facial expressions. Thus, this cultural difference cannot be attributed to cultural differences in the emotion words used in the study.

There was, however, one minor loophole that still existed concerning this finding. In Ekman's (1972) original universality research, judgments of intensity were obtained from Japanese, Americans, Chileans, Argentinians, and Brazilians. They reported at that time that they found no cultural differences in the intensity judgments. We reanalyzed the original intensity judgment data, suspecting that the earlier non-findings were products of artifacts in the statistical variances associated with the data (heterogeneity of the variability in the ratings across the cultures would throw off the statistical analyses using these data). In comparing only the American and Japanese data, there were indeed cultural differences in the intensity ratings in these data as well, with the Japanese giving lower ratings (reported in Matsumoto, 1986).

These findings have again been replicated in yet another study since (Matsumoto, 1991). Thus, we are confident at this time that the Japanese judge facial expressions of emotion with less intensity than do Americans.

Japanese Perceptions of Smiles

The smile is an important expression in the Japanese culture. Smiles are the most common mask of emotion. Japanese people, like many other people of the world, are often in situations that require them to hide or conceal their true, often negative, feelings. In these situations, the Japanese will most likely smile. It is also not uncommon for the Japanese to simulate positive feelings by smiling, that is, showing that they feel positive even when they are not.

The special place of the smile in the Japanese culture is related to the Japanese culture's emphasis on collectiveness and status differentiation. In Japan, the uninhibited expression of inappropriate emotions toward others can violate cultural norms dictating the suppression of these emotions. If these emotions are expressed, they can threaten either interpersonal relationships or the preservation of status differences. Smiling serves to maintain relationships, or to subordinate oneself to others of higher status. Thus, it is very important for the individual Japanese not only to learn what these rules are but also to know instinctively how to apply them; the expert use of the smile serves as an important social glue in the Japanese culture. When smiles are used in this fashion, they become signs of something other than true joy, or happiness, or positive emotion. Accordingly, Japanese people learn that the smile does not necessarily mean that one is happy.

The use of smiles in the Japanese culture can be contrasted to their use in other cultures more individualistic and less status differentiating, in which there are fewer social and cultural norms that dictate the concealing of one's true feelings. American culture, for example, for the most part encourages its members to express emotions freely and without sanction. People have less need to use smiles as a mask, so that when they smile, it is more often a sign of genuine joy, or at least pleasure—the quality being measured by the broadness of the smile.

One interesting example of anecdotal evidence about the differential use of smiles is found in photographs. In the United States, it is common practice for people posing for photographs to smile (cheese): the smile is associated with positive meaning, which the poser intends to project in the photograph. In Japan, however, it is more common to see posers with a neutral or serious expression. This is due, at least in part, to the different meaning that the smile has acquired in the Japanese culture. The Japanese learn that smiles are not necessarily associated with positive emotion. In fact, posed smiles may easily be associated with negative emotion, and are more offensive than pleasant (although this trend seems to be changing with younger Japanese of today).

Because smiles are used differently in the Japanese culture, smiles should be interpreted differently. Japanese people should interpret smiles as showing less intense emotion than Westerners, because smiles are used more often as signs of something other than true joy or happiness. When Westerners see others smile, they will attribute greater intensity of emotion to the smile, because smiles are used more often as signs of true positive emotion.

In order to test this idea, we compiled all the emotion intensity judgments gathered from different cultures in different studies on the eight smile expressions in the JACFEE. Respondents came from the United States, Vietnam, Indonesia, Poland, Hungary, India, and Japan. Each of the cultures was assigned culture scores for individualism and status differentiation, derived from Hofstede's (1980, 1983) cross-cultural value survey. When we correlated the culture scores with the emotion intensity judgments, we found that collective cultures such as Japan attributed lower emotion intensity to the smiles than individualistic cultures such as the U.S. We also found that cultures high in status differentiation, such as Japan, attributed lower emotion intensities to the smiles.

Smiles are also unique because judgments other than that of emotion are inferred on the basis of smiles. It is common, for example, for people to make judgments of attractiveness, intelligence, friendliness, sociability, and the like on the basis of smiles. The Japanese culture may influence these kinds of judgments, in addition to attributions of emotion intensity. Because individualistic, low status differentiating cultures attribute greater emotion intensity to smiles, they may also foster more positive judgments on other dimensions. If this were true, Americans should judge smiling persons to be more attractive, more intelligent, or more sociable than Japanese observers. The Japanese, on the other hand, should have less positive evaluations of smiles.

We (Matsumoto & Kudoh, 1993) tested this idea by showing American and Japanese respondents photographs of Caucasian and Japanese posers expressing both smiles and neutral faces. Respondents rated each photograph on four different social dimensions: attractiveness, intelligence, friendliness, and sociability. We originally chose these dimensions because previous writers (e.g., Ekman, 1978) suggested that they are some of the more salient and obvious social dimensions that are inferred on the basis of facial expressions.

We were interested in finding out how the Japanese differed from the Americans in several ways. First, we compared both cultures' judgments of smiles against their own judgments of neutral faces. The Americans judged smiles more favorably in all comparisons against neutral faces; the Japanese did not. This finding highlighted the differences between smiles and neutral faces in both cultures. In another comparison, we tested the judgments of the Americans and the Japanese against each other, first for smiles and then again for neutrals. For smiles, the Americans had more positive ratings than the Japanese; on the neutral faces, there was no difference between the two cultures. Again, this finding highlights the differences between smiles and neutrals in the U.S. and Japan.

In order to explore the possible bases for these differences, we compared the four ratings against themselves, separately for Americans and Japanese. For Americans, the attractiveness dimension made the largest contribution to their overall judgments. For the Japanese, the most salient dimension was intelligence. The Japanese made judgments about qualities internal to the posers, whereas the Americans appear to have been making judgments about qualities external to the posers. This finding suggests yet another difference between the processes by which the Japanese and Americans make judgments of others' smiles.

The findings from the studies presented in this section indicate clearly that the Japanese interpret smiles differently from non-Japanese. These differences in interpretation arise because of differences in the actual use of smiles in everyday social interaction. Compared with Americans, the Japanese not only perceive less emotion in the smiles of others, they also judge them less positively. Also, when making social judgments of others, the dimensions that contribute most to the Japanese interpretations are different from the dimensions contributing to American judgments.

Understanding Japanese Cultural Differences in Emotional Perception: Decoding Rules

The evidence provided in this chapter is clear regarding Japanese perceptions of emotion. The Japanese are similar to people of other cultures in that they have the ability to perceive exactly the same facial expressions of emotion that others perceive. But the Japanese are unique in that their culture produces differences in the degree to which they use this ability, in the degree of intensity they attribute to the expressions of others, in the interpretation of smiles, and in social judgments.

How is it that the Japanese perception of emotion can be universal and at the same time unique? Cultural display rules provide one explanation. The human brain stores detailed information concerning the exact facial muscle configurations of the universal emotions. Ekman (1972) coined the term Facial Affect Program to refer to the storage of this information. When emotion is triggered, a message is sent to the Facial Affect Program to signal emotion on the face. The Facial Affect Program sends the information about the appropriate facial muscle configuration to the face, but before reaching the face, this signal is joined with signals coming from areas of the brain that store information concerning cultural display rules. The display rules may then alter the original signal from the Facial Affect Program. The resulting joint output is then sent to the face, and the expression that occurs is the result of this cojoint process between the Facial Affect Program and cultural display rules.

This process may be occurring for emotional perception as well. When a visual stimulus (someone else's facial expression) is received, its sensory message may be sent to an area of the brain, much like the Facial Affect Program, that stores information concerning the facial configurations of the universal emotions. Here, the sensory information may be matched with templates of each of the universal emotions, which I call the Facial Affect Recognition Program. A message is then sent to another area of the brain where classification and interpretation concerning the stimulus will occur. Before reaching its endpoint in judgment, however, the original message combines with learned information about how to interpret emotional expressions appropriately depending on social circumstance. This information is called *decoding rules*, and much like display rules, these are social and cultural conventions concerning the appropriate interpretations of others' behavior. Thus, the final judgment produced concerning an external stimulus represents the interaction between universal, biologically innate mechanisms storing the templates of universal facial emotion, and culturally learned decoding rules (see Figure 6).

Research has not yet specified the exact areas of the brain where these processes may be occurring, but unpublished findings from studies in Europe, for example, have suggested that there are direct, neural pathways from the retina to areas of the lower brain that do not connect to higher association areas of the brain. Other psychological theories of perception include similar mechanisms involving "bottom-up" and "top-down" modes of processing. Future research will explore these theories and specify exactly the neural pathways that are involved in these activities.

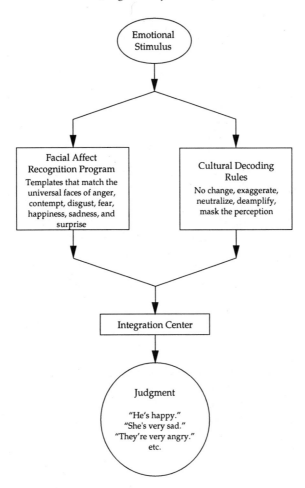

Fig. 6. A Process Model of Emotional Perception with Decoding Rules

How early in life do the Japanese learn these rules? There have been numerous studies in the United States on children's and infant's perceptions of facial expressions of emotion. These studies have repeatedly shown that infants attend to universal facial expressions differently from other, nonemotional stimuli and that, by childhood, judgments of emotion are relatively stable and consistent with judgments made by adults. I know of no study, however, that has compared Japanese children's or infant's perceptions with those of children from other cultures. Almost ten years ago, we did compare Japanese and American children's perceptions of vocal expressions of emotion (Matsumoto & Kishimoto, 1983). These findings suggested that, even in children as young as three years old, there were considerable differences in the recognition accuracies between the two cultures. My guess is that Japanese children start learning decoding and display rules from day one of life, and that most of these rules are internalized by childhood.

This chapter has explored the ways in which the Japanese are similar to and different from people of other cultures in their perceptions of the emotions of others. The evidence given here clearly reflects how Japanese culture and society influence how Japanese people perceive the world. These findings are important because other research has demonstrated that how one perceives others has a direct and substantial influence on one's own emotional experiences and emotional expressions. This information also has direct practical ramifications to social interaction, in that it gives us a basis for understanding cultural differences in the interpretations of the behavior of others. Just as emotional expressions may be variable according to social context, emotion judgments may also be variable, and the interpretation processes of the Japanese may be similar to or different from those of non-Japanese, depending on the nature of that context. The next chapter examines the ways in which the language and concept of emotion in Japan are similar to, and different from, those of other cultures of the world.

Chapter 7

The Concepts and Language
of Emotion in Japan

The preceding chapters have focused on how different components of emotions of the Japanese are similar to or different from those of non-Japanese. These components have included such topics as the expression of emotion, emotional perception, the antecedents and elicitors to emotion, cognitive evaluations of antecedent events, and display rules. Although most cross-cultural research on emotions in Japan has focused on these components of emotion, it has not yet considered another central question about possible Japanese cultural differences in emotion—that is, whether the concept of "emotion" means the same thing in Japan as it does elsewhere, and whether the word emotion itself means the same in the Japanese language as it does in other languages.

The study of emotion via the language of a culture is important and necessary in gaining an understanding of emotion in that culture. Cultures will differ in their vocabularies of emotion—in the number of words, and their uses and meanings. These differences can point to important differences in the ways by which people of different cultures construct their emotional worlds using their language. By examining these culturally related constructions in language, we can gain yet another glimpse of the emotional world of the Japanese.

Such an examination must be done carefully, avoiding false assumptions. It is easy to conclude, for example, that cultural differences in the meanings and uses of emotion words across cultures suggest that the emotions themselves are totally different across cultures. Just because a culture may not have a word for an emotion we know in English does not necessarily mean that the people of that culture do not experience that emotion. The anthropologist Robert Levy (1984), for instance, has suggested that the Tahitians do not have a word that corresponds to the English word sadness. Yet, he has observed Tahitians expressing sadness in their facial expressions, in other overt behaviors, and in their speech about sadness-producing events. He concludes that even though the Tahitian language may not have an equivalent for the English word sadness, the Tahitians still apparently feel and express this emotion in their everyday lives. Thus, it is not necessarily the presence or absence of emotion terminology per se that is important; rather, it is the philosophy underlying that presence or absence in terms of the social meanings and social constructions of reality that should be the focus of our interest. That is, we should be able to obtain glimpses of how a culture constructs reality by the way it identifies and labels concepts via language. It is with this caveat that we must approach understanding the concept and language of emotion in Japan.

In this chapter, we examine how Japanese culture and language represent the concept of emotion. The material presented will shed more light on how Japanese culture and society mold the emotional experiences of its members. Before presenting the cross-cultural research conducted to date on this topic, however, it is useful to contrast how traditional, Western science views the concept of emotion. This presentation should provide a basis of comparison by which to interpret the Japanese emotion lexicon.

Traditional Views of Emotion in Western Psychology

When American psychologists, and the lay public, think and speak of "emotion," one aspect of emotion generally comes to mind: the subjective, inner feeling states of emotion. In fact, this focus on the subjective, inner experience of emotional states has characterized how Western, and American, psychology generally thinks about, and studies, emotion and emotion-related phenomena.

One of the oldest theories of emotion in Western psychology is the James-Lange theory (Lange & James, 1922). This theory suggests

that the conscious experience of emotion results from one's perception of autonomic arousal and overt behavior. Thus, you may see a
bear and run; your interpretation of your running (and breathing,
and heart rate, etc.) produces the emotional experience of fear. On
the other hand, the Cannon-Bard (Bard, 1934; Cannon, 1927) theory
of emotion argued that autonomic arousal was too slow to account
for changes in emotional experience, and proposed that emotional
experience resulted from direct stimulation of brain centers in the
cortex that produced the conscious experience of emotion. The more
recent Schachter-Singer (1962) theory of emotion focuses on the role
of cognitive interpretation. It suggests that emotional experiences
need not be differentiated according to autonomic arousal or behavior; instead, what is important in the production of conscious emotional experience is one's interpretation of the environment in which
one is being aroused. Emotion therefore results from the labeling of
the arousal or behavior in that situation.

Other important theories of emotion focus on the expression of
emotion. In general, these theories argue that emotions are evolutionarily adaptive, and that their expression is biologically innate and
universal to all people of all cultures and races. Some of the major
proponents of these theories are Tomkins, Izard, Plutchik, and Ekman. These writers cite studies documenting the universal expression
and recognition of facial expressions of emotion as evidence for this
point of view (the same evidence reviewed in Chapter 2). But even
though these theories focus on the expression of emotion, they gain
their importance in Western and American psychology because of
their meaning to inner, subjective experience. The word "expression" itself signifies such importance, since emotional expressions
are, by definition, outward signals of more important inner, emotional states. The study of expression in Western psychology is fueled
in part by Western scientists' belief in the importance of the inner,
subjective feelings that are being expressed.

There is thus a considerable degree of agreement in Western psychology about the importance of introspective, personal experience,
and what we call that experience (i.e., emotion labeling). What emotion is, and what we call it, define emotion as being private and personal phenomena that have meaning to us as separate identities.

This view of emotion probably makes good, intuitive sense to many of us, especially American readers, but it may be a particularly Western, or even more specifically an American, way of understanding emotion. Certainly, although there is some similarity between American and Japanese views of emotion itself, there are also a good many differences.

Research on the Concepts and Language of Emotion in Japan

The question of concepts and language of emotion, spanning not only the Japanese language and culture, but also many other cultures and languages in the world, has been studied by anthropologists and social psychologists alike, and has involved cultures familiar to the lay public (e.g., France, Germany, Japan, China), as well as some unfamiliar ones (e.g., the Ifaluk of Micronesia, the Chewong of Malay, the Bimin-Kuskusmin of Papua, New Guinea). An excellent review of these studies was written by Russell (1991) and is the basis for some of the material reviewed here.

Of course, we are most concerned in this book about the concept and vocabulary of emotion in Japan. Fortunately, there has been a number of studies, conducted by both Japanese and American researchers, that speak to these issues. Some studies have examined a wide range of Japanese emotion words, while others have focused on one or two specific emotions. A common technique has been to obtain similarity ratings among pairs of Japanese emotion words by Japanese respondents, and then to subject these ratings to the technique of multidimensional scaling, by which the similarities between emotion words are expressed on a two-dimensional plane and then compared with planes obtained in different cultures (e.g., Russell, 1983; Yoshida, Kinase, Kurokawa, & Yashiro, 1970).

Another technique that has been used obtains ratings of specific emotion words in the Japanese language on semantic differential scales. The semantic differential items are typically chosen because they allow for an empirical definition of the semantic meanings of the emotion words. The ratings obtained on the Japanese words are usually compared with those obtained on English equivalents of the same words (Imada, 1989; Imada, Araki, & Kujime, 1991; Tanaka-Matsumi & Marsella, 1977). Yet another type of study reported in the literature has involved the use of free associations of respondents to various emotion words in Japan, and the comparison of these associations with those of respondents in the United States (Tanaka-Matsumi & Marsella, 1976). Another study compared the associations to emotion words in Japanese with associations obtained from respondents in China to the same words (Chan, 1990).

To compare the results of these various studies, spanning many different emotion words in the Japanese language, and utilizing a variety of different methodologies, the following section examines in turn different aspects of the vocabulary of emotion in Japan, and how they may be similar to, or different from, those in other cultures and languages. For reference, I have tried to present findings from unfamiliar as well as familiar cultures. These findings provide us with interesting and provocative information about how the Japanese construct their emotional words via their language.

Differences in Defining and Understanding Emotions in Japan

THE CONCEPT AND DEFINITION OF EMOTION

When we discuss human emotions in American psychology, we often presuppose that what we are talking about is the same for all people. Studies spanning many different cultures suggest that emotion is a universal concept; but not all cultures have a specific word for emotion, or even a concept of emotion—though they feel emotions. Levy (1973, 1984), for example, suggests that Tahitians do not have a word for emotion. Lutz (1982, 1983) suggests that the Ifaluks of Micronesia do not have a word for emotion. Gerber (1975, reported in Russell, 1991) suggests that the Samoans do not have a word for emotion, but do have a word (*lagona*) that refers to feelings and sensations. Brandt and Boucher (1986), on the other hand, studied the concepts of depression in eight different cultures, involving the Indonesian, Japanese, Korean, Malaysian, Spanish, and Sinhalese languages. Before conducting the study, collaborators in each of the cultures assured the researchers that each of the languages had a word for emotion, suggesting the cross-cultural equivalence in the concept of emotion.

The Japanese language has several words that express the concept of emotion—for example, *kanjo* and *jodo*—but it is not clear that the concept thus expressed embraces the same states of feeling as the English word emotion. Matsuyama, Hama, Kawamura, and Mine (1978) conducted a study of emotion words in Japan that involved the rating of many different words, some of them with clear correspondences as emotion words in the English language, such as angry and sad; others, however, though emotion words in Japanese, would not be so regarded in English—considerate, lucky, motivated, calculating. Russell's (1983) study also included a number of words in Japanese that may or may not coincide with what might be considered emotion— at ease, aroused, bored, sleepy, tired.

The confusion among emotion words across different cultures is not surprising, considering that even within any one culture there can be multiple words to represent emotion and emotion-related phenomena, each overlapping to varying degrees: in the English language, for example, emotion, feeling, sensation, affect. Consider on top of that all the various synonyms for each of the specific emotions that we have in English. Other studies also suggest that not all people in the world have a word referring to the English concept of emotion, and that not all concepts of emotion are equivalent.

THE CATEGORIZATION OR LABELING OF EMOTION

Just as there are cultural similarities and differences in the concepts and definitions of emotion, there are similarities and differences in the way in which cultures classify different emotional feelings via their language labels. Certainly, many English words find equivalents in the Japanese language and culture, such as anger, joy, sadness, liking, loving, and so on. Most emotion words probably do have equivalents in the Japanese language, underscoring a great degree of similarity in the construction of emotional experience in Japan. But there are several English words that have no equivalent in Japanese, and there are Japanese words that have no exact English equivalent. For example, the Japanese words *itoshii, ijirashii, amae,* and *sunao* have no exact English translation and can only be described as concepts: roughly, as longing for an absent loved one, a feeling associated with seeing someone praiseworthy overcoming an obstacle, dependence, and sincerity and compliance, respectively. Likewise, there are some English words that have no exact equivalents in the Japanese, or have been assimilated into the Japanese language only recently; to be annoyed, at ease, or comfortable are some examples. Also, the English concept of guilt carries connotations that do not readily translate in the Japanese.

Similar discrepancies come to mind for other cultures and languages. For example, there is no exact English translation for the German word *schadenfreude*, which refers to pleasure derived from another's misfortunes. Leff (1973) pointed out that some African languages have a word that covers what the English suggests are two emotions—anger and sadness. Likewise, Lutz (1982) suggests that the Ifaluk word *song* can be described sometimes as anger, and sometimes as sadness. Some English words have no equivalents in other languages. Hiatt (1978), for example, suggests that the English words terror, horror, dread, apprehension, and timidity are all referred to by a single word in Gigjingali, an Australian aboriginal language (*gurakadj*). This aboriginal word also refers to the English concepts of shame and fear. Frustration may be a word with no exact equivalent in Arabic languages (Russell, 1991).

These differences in the presence or absence of different emotion words are extremely important to understanding how the Japanese culture, via its language, attempts to structure and understand the emotional world of the Japanese people. Students of Japanese culture will be quick to recognize the importance of such words as *sunao*, or *amae* to the Japanese culture and the psychology of the Japanese people. These words find no exact English translations, but their existence in the Japanese language allows the Japanese people to label and identify aspects of their emotional worlds, which reinforces their importance in the Japanese culture. By labeling these concepts, Japanese culture and language identify and recognize the importance of these concepts to the culture and psychology of people. The relationship between language and culture is reciprocal: these labels reinforce culture just as culture reinforces these labels.

In contrast, consider a language such as English that has no exact equivalent of these words. If the language cannot readily identify and label those emotions or situations via a single word, the concepts themselves and their importance in the culture remain unclear. It is true that in the American culture, the concepts and feelings that underlie the Japanese words *amae* and *sunao* certainly do exist, but they do not play the same role in the American culture as they do in the Japanese culture, nor do they have the same meanings even when they do occur in the American culture. These studies, and many others like them, suggest that every culture has its distinct concepts of emotion, and its own distinct ways of framing and labeling its emotion world.

THE LOCATION OF EMOTION

One of the most important components of emotion according to American psychology is the inner, subjective experience of emotion. But the importance placed on one's inner feelings, and the importance of introspection (i.e., looking inside oneself) may itself be culture bound by American psychology. The Japanese culture can, and does, view emotions as originating or residing somewhere else. In the United States, we place matters of emotion and inner feelings in a single bodily location—the heart. Although the Japanese culture is similar in some respects, with its referents to the heart, or *kokoro*, the Japanese also identify many of their emotion referents in the *hara*, translated as the gut or abdomen. The common American expression "gut feeling," meaning visceral, is similar, though the plural noun guts, as in "has a lot of guts," connotes pluck or nerve.

Other cultures differ as well. For example, emotion words in the languages of several Oceanic peoples, such as the Samoans (Gerber, 1975, reported in Russell, 1991), Pintupi Aborigines (Myers, 1979), and Solomon Islanders (White, 1980), are statements about the relationship between a person and an event, rather than matters of personal or individual feelings. Likewise, Riesman (1977) suggests that the central African Fulani's concept of *semteende*, which is commonly translated as shame or embarrassment, refers more to a situation than to a feeling. That is, someone is in a state of *semteende* if the situation is appropriate to *semteende*, regardless of what one feels. The Chewong of Malay group feelings and thoughts in the liver (Howell, 1981). Levy (1984) argues that in Tahitian thinking, emotions arise from the intestines. Lutz (1982) suggests that the closest Ifaluk word to the English "emotion" was *niferash*, which she translated as "our insides."

CULTURAL DIFFERENCES IN THE MEANING OF EMOTIONS TO PEOPLE AND TO BEHAVIOR

Emotions have enormous personal and individual meaning in American psychology and culture, perhaps because American psychology views inner, subjective feelings as the major defining characteristic of emotion. In the United States, we place much importance on how we feel. Emotions are given a special and important place in the American culture. We value the feelings of others, even children, and make special efforts to evaluate those feelings when making major decisions. Defining emotions in such a way means that the major purpose of emotion is to help define one's unique individuality; one's self-definitions, that is, the ways by which one defines and identifies oneself, are all influenced by one's emotions, because they are personal, private, inner experiences.

The Japanese think of emotions in a different way, because of differences in emotion concepts, location, and labeling. Emotions are not afforded the personal, individual importance they receive in the American culture. Rather, individual feelings and introspection have importance more for one's place in society, and in everyday social interaction. The Japanese concept of *amae*, for example, which is typically considered a central emotional topic in Japanese culture, specifies an interdependent relationship between two people, not a special feeling state with meaning only for one person.

Even emotions that are typically considered basic in American psychology have different social meanings and connotations in the Japanese culture. Anger, for example, is important in the Japanese culture not because of its intense, personal meanings to oneself but because of what it implies about one's relationships with others, and how those relationships may change in the future. In the same way, joy or happiness is not solely a representation of inner, self-pleasure; rather, it may reflect a statement of the successful resolution or outcome in relation to one's relationship with others, such as the successful fulfillment of social obligations.

The Japanese culture is not the only culture that considers emotions to be statements of the relationship between people and their environment, be it things in the environment, or social relationships with other people. Emotions for both the Ifaluks of Micronesia (Lutz, 1982) and the Tahitians (Levy, 1984), for instance, denote statements of social relationships and the physical environment. The definition of emotion as primarily a matter of self-introspection and personal feeling is predominant only in American psychology. To be sure, views of emotion as social constructions have not been totally absent in American psychology (e.g., Averill, 1975), but they have received considerably less attention in mainstream, academic psychology than views that center on the introspection of subjective feeling states. This bias in academic circles is probably a reflection of the inherent cultural bias we share concerning our definition of emotion as an individual, personal phenomenon.

TRANSLATION EQUIVALENCE

Needless to say, all these differences in our concepts and language of emotion present special problems in the translation of emotion words. In fact, one can question whether exact translation equivalents are even possible. Several studies have examined this question with respect to the Japanese language. In one study, Tanaka-Matsumi and Marsella (1976), using back-translation procedures and a dictionary to find the best equivalent of the English word for depression in the Japanese language, finally settled on the word *yuutsu*. They then compared the free associations given by English speakers to the word depression with those given by Japanese speakers to *yuutsu*. The associations were quite different. In another study, Tanaka-Matsumi and Marsella (1977) asked subjects to rate depression and *yuutsu* on semantic differential scales. Separate analyses for the terms yielded different factor structures.

Studies conducted by Imada (1989; Imada, Araki, & Kujime, 1991) came to similar conclusions concerning depression/*yuutsu*, fear/*kyofu*, and anxiety/*fuan*. It is very likely that studies of other pairs of emotion words between Japanese and English (or other languages) would yield similarly conflicting results.

Implications of our Understanding of Emotions in Japan and Across Other Cultures

Although emotion is a concept universal to all human beings, our understanding of it is very dependent on the language that we have available to describe it. In turn, the language that we use to describe our emotion worlds helps to define those worlds for us. Thus, culture shapes and molds language, and language, in turn, reinforces the cultures from which it originates. By analyzing the language of emotion in a culture we can further our understanding, and appreciation, of the feelings and emotions of the people of that culture.

There is no question that there is a considerable amount of overlap and similarity in the emotion vocabulary between the Japanese and English (American) languages. Many emotion words in English find equivalents in the Japanese language, and vice versa. When American psychologists study such emotions as anger, contempt, disgust, fear, happiness, sadness, and surprise in Japan, we find that we can easily translate these words into Japanese (e.g., *ikari, keibetsu, iyake, osore, yorokobi, kanashimi,* and *odoroki,* respectively). If we ask observers in Japan to label facial expressions with these response alternatives, they will give the same type of data that American observers, or other observers around the world, will. If we ask respondents in Japan to tell us about the last time they felt each of these emotions, they will be able to do so, with little or no difficulty, just as respondents in many other cultures will. These overwhelming similarities point out the many universal aspects of these types of human emotions to people of all different cultures.

Yet, although there are fewer differences than similarities between the English and Japanese emotion lexicons, they are important ones, particularly in terms of our attempts at further understanding the emotion worlds of the Japanese. Differences in the emotion lexicons give us important glimpses into how Japanese culture and society, via language, help individual members construct their emotional experiences. By examining these constructions, we can begin to see how the Japanese view emotions, the meaning of emotion to individual Japanese, and the role of emotion in Japanese culture and society.

THE SOCIAL ROLES OF EMOTION IN THE JAPANESE EMOTION LEXICON

In comparison with the emotion lexicon in English, the vocabulary of emotion in Japan is much less a private, personal statement of one's inner, subjective feelings. Instead, it encompasses much more a statement concerning the status of one's relationship with others. Several points discussed earlier in this chapter bear this out. For example, the Japanese word *amae,* which has received a good deal of attention in the psychological literature as a key element of the psychology of the Japanese, refers to one's dependence on another. Doi (1973) suggests that this emotional concept is one of the most important concepts in Japan because it captures the basic elements of social interrelatedness and social interdependence that the Japanese have among each other. Indeed this fostering of bonds between people and among groups is a key element of Japanese culture and society, which is manifested in the individual psychology of the Japanese, their emotion worlds, and their language.

Sunao, roughly translated as feelings of sincerity or humility, has similar connections with the social hierarchy in that it refers to one's actions of compliance toward others, especially those of higher status. Again, these feelings, and the behavior associated with them, are important for the individual Japanese because they help to maintain the social order that is essential for the harmony, indeed the survival, of the Japanese culture and people as we have come to know them.

There are important cultural differences in the social meanings of more basic emotion words also. One important examples is *ikari,* the Japanese word for anger. When one says that one is angry in Japan, it is as much a statement of the state of one's relationship with others as it is a statement of one's personal feelings about something. The specific meaning of the statement, moreover, can vary depending on the social context. If one joins others in expressing anger at an outgroup, for instance, the sharing of the anger helps to foster ingroup bonds. But if one expresses anger at someone within one's ingroup, the anger threatens the ingroup bonds. In some senses, it is also conceivable that those bonds are already being broken.

Emotions in the English language can, and often do, have the same kinds of effects on social relationships. Expressions of anger in the situations described above may produce the same results on social bonds. The difference between the social meanings of the Japanese and English languages is therefore not so much a matter of totally different meanings, rather, it is a difference in the degree of meaning between social impact and personal expression. In this light, it is clear that the emotion language of the Japanese places much more emphasis on the social meanings of emotion than does the English language.

THE PERSONAL MEANINGS OF EMOTION
IN THE JAPANESE EMOTION LEXICON

That the Japanese place emotions in the *hara,* or gut, speaks to the importance of emotions in Japanese culture and society, and to Japanese people. In Japanese culture, and as expressed in many Eastern philosophies, one's soul and spirit are located in the gut. Life energy, translated in the Japanese as *ki*, is found in the gut. In many ways, the gut is revered in Japan, and honored in the Japanese language by many phrases and idioms that refer to important emotions (e.g., *hara ga tatsu*—literally, "my gut stands," which means "I am angry"; *hara ga dekita hito*—literally, "a person who has developed gut, which refers to a person with strong moral character). It is also interesting to note the association between emotions, the gut, and the suicide ritual of *harakiri* or *seppuku*, that is, self-disembowelment by cutting one's gut by one's own hand. Despite the overtly grotesque nature of this ritual, it came to be interpreted as an act of honor in feudal Japan, an image supported until this day via the mass media, television shows, and movies.

I believe that the Japanese are intensely emotional people, and that inner, subjective experiences—feelings—are extremely important to them; but because the language of emotion has so many different connotations in Japan, many Japanese people avoid direct statements about their personal feelings. This has to do, in particular, with the social meanings of emotions in Japan, and the effects emotions have on social relationships. Because of these possible effects, the Japanese are much more reserved than Americans in their statements involving emotions.

Unfortunately, this reticence has led many observers, both scholarly and lay, to conclude that emotions are not important in the Japanese culture, or to the Japanese people. We tend to overlook the fact that, as with nonverbal displays such as facial expressions (Chapter 3), the Japanese must also monitor their verbal expressions. To outsiders, the Japanese may be cold, emotionless and expressionless beings; to insiders, the Japanese are intensely emotional people.

In some senses, the emotion lexicon of the Japanese places an added burden on the individual Japanese, who must weigh the consequences and meanings of the expression of important, personal feelings to social relationships. The differential degrees of social meanings to the Japanese, via their language, make it much more difficult for them to express emotion or feeling; they have neither the social freedom nor the vocabulary to express such things in the way that Americans can, who speak freely about their emotions in the rich English language with its many shades of meaning. Emotions in general, and the language of emotion in particular, hold special places in the lives and culture of the Japanese.

Conclusions

This chapter has discussed how the concepts and meanings of the term emotion in Japan are similar to, and different from, the emotion lexicons in the United States and elsewhere. Although traditional studies on human emotion in psychology have generally focused on the experience, perception, or expression of emotion, an understanding of the vocabulary of emotion in the Japanese language is important to an understanding of the emotional worlds of the Japanese. The many similarities between Japanese and English, and the several important differences, give us ways in which we can come to understand how Japanese culture and society mold the emotion worlds of the Japanese people through language. Also, we can see how the Japanese language defines the individual emotions of its people in ways that matter to the survival and maintenance of the culture.

One important field of investigation that was not reviewed in this chapter concerns the expression of emotions and emotion-related thoughts and feelings via speech and communication styles. There is a considerable literature on intercultural communication featuring Japanese discourse patterns that relate to this issue (e.g., Barnlund, 1975; Gudykunst, 1991; Gudykunst & Nishida, 1994). In general, these studies have shown that the Japanese tend to be less self-revealing in their speech and language than Westerners, particularly in the use of expressions of intimacy and personal feeling. This chapter was limited to reviews of literature relating to concepts of emotion, but these other aspects of emotion-related communication and language also speak to the important ways in which the Japanese culture structures and divides the emotional words of the Japanese people.

The next chapter discusses ways of understanding culture in general that will help to deepen our understanding of the Japanese culture in particular, and tie together many of the pieces so far presented.

Chapter 8

Meaningful Dimensions of Cultural Variability in Japan

*Improving Our Conceptual Understanding
of the Japanese Culture and Its Impact
on Emotion*

Different studies on the culture, society, and people of any nation will inevitably produce varied findings—some of which, in large programs of research, are in conflict with each other. In cross-cultural research in particular, these conflicts often involve findings demonstrating cultural similarities or universalities on one hand, and cultural differences or specifics on the other. This is no less true for Japanese culture and society. As we have seen in the last six chapters, there are numerous examples of how Japanese concepts of emotion are similar to, and at the same time different from, those of other cultures. There are similarities as well as differences in facial expressions, in emotional experience, antecedents and elicitors of emotion, the cognitive evaluation of emotion antecedents, the perception of emotion, and the concepts and language of emotion. And, most importantly, both the similarities and differences speak to important aspects of the Japanese culture, and guide us in understanding the emotions and feelings of the Japanese people.

Still, it is not enough simply to produce facts. The mere production of facts in study after study really does not add much to our understanding of emotions in Japan unless the facts are accompanied by a conceptual framework within which they can be understood, and predicted. In other words, we need a theoretical model of the emo-

tions and feelings of the Japanese—a way of understanding our findings—that will encompass both the similarities and differences that
we have uncovered in our studies.

This chapter presents such a theoretical framework. The framework involves two meaningful dimensions of cultural variability—
individualism-collectivism (IC) and status differentiation (SD)—that
can be used to understand all cultures and societies, not only the
Japanese. This framework can, I think, be used to account for much
of the findings we have obtained to date across our various studies.
More importantly, this framework can also be used to provide more
predictions about Japanese cultural influences on emotion in comparative research across cultures in the future. Before describing this
framework, it is useful to review some traditional theoretical frame-
works of understanding cultural similarities and differences in Japan.

Traditional Views of the Japanese Culture

Scholars have produced many credible and influential reports of
the behaviors of the Japanese people, and the cultural forces at work
to influence those behaviors, and many of these have been developed
from a variety of research paradigms. These paradigms have involved
different disciplines and methodologies and have included simple observations and personal reflection (e.g., Reischauer, 1988), in-depth
anthropological ethnographies (e.g., Benedict, 1946), studies in communication patterns (e.g., Barnlund, 1975), psychiatric and clinical
observations and interventions (e.g., Doi, 1973, 1985), and systematic
psychological studies like those described earlier in this book.

All these approaches differ in at least two respects—that is, how
data were collected, and how the data were interpreted. All these approaches have been useful in fostering our understanding and appreciation of the Japanese people and culture, at least in terms of the data
that were collected, and I do not at all mean to suggest that data obtained from one approach are better or worse than others: all data,
from all these approaches, have contributed not only to our understanding of Japan but also to our scientific approaches to the study of
Japan.

At the same time, we must address serious questions about how
we have come to understand the people and culture of Japan and

about how we have developed our conceptual models to incorporate this understanding. In most cases, the interpretation of the data— that is, the development of conceptual and theoretical ways of understanding the Japanese—has been strongly influenced by personal anecdote, impression, or stereotype. These are useful, but students of Japan need to give serious consideration to the development of theoretical models that have a more solid, scientifically reliable base. We need to search for meaningful ways of describing the Japanese culture that will help us to understand and predict both cultural similarities and differences in emotion, and also allow us to understand the Japanese culture in relation to other cultures. This underlying philosophy necessitates the search for a framework or methodology that is based on meaningful dimensions of cultural variability and is applicable to all cultures in general.

The Search for Meaningful Dimensions of Cultural Variability

As our findings concerning cultural differences in various emotion components in the Japanese began to increase in number and complexity, we were forced to confront the problem of understanding these similarities and differences. Moreover, we were forced not only to understand these similarities and differences in relation to the Japanese culture but also, because our research program often included people of multiple cultures, to consider how we could find and use dimensions of cultural variability that were meaningful to all the cultures we studied and could produce specific, predictable hypotheses about cultural differences in emotion. If we could specify such important dimensions of culture, then we would be able to understand not just Japanese culture and society but other cultures as well. Basing our work in panculturally relevant dimensions, rather than culture-specific anecdotes or impressions, was important for lifting not only our work but this type of cross-cultural research in general to a more perceptive level of scientific philosophy.

The development of panculturally relevant dimensions of cultural variability is necessary not only from the standpoint of science and philosophy. Indeed, it is becoming increasingly important in today's multicultural, multiracial, pluralistic world. Especially here in the United States, people of many different racial, ethnic, and cultural backgrounds live in close proximity to each other. There is no doubt that acceptance and recognition of cultural differences can lead to a rich and rewarding sphere of professional and personal activities, yet it is also true that cultural differences and misunderstandings have the potential to contribute to tension, mistrust, and at times, violence. These are major problems facing many nations of the world, not only the United States. Interracial marriages and advanced technologies that enable instant communication across the globe make it additionally clear to us that we must search for meaningful, pan-cultural dimensions of cultural variability, and use these dimensions in our attempts to understand, and interact with, people of differing racial and cultural backgrounds.

Fortunately, the social science literature, both in anthropology and psychology, contains many examples of cross-cultural dimensions, some of which were based in ethnographic studies of Japan. Of these, perhaps the most relevant and often-cited dimension is that known as Individualism vs. collectivism (IC—Hofstede, 1980, 1983; Kluckholn & Strodbeck, 1961; Mead, 1967; Triandis, 1972), which refers to the degree to which cultures encourage individual needs, wishes, desires, and values in relation to group and collective ones. Individualistic cultures encourage their members to be unique; individual goals, values, behaviors, and self-expression take precedence over collective needs of groups or others. Individualistic cultures foster a sense of self that is independent, autonomous, and clearly separate from others (Markus & Kitayama, 1991).

Collective cultures, by contrast, emphasize the needs of groups, and individual goals are subordinated to group goals. Individual identification in collective cultures comes through group affiliation. Conformity, compliance, and cooperation within groups is emphasized. Collective cultures tend to foster a sense of self that is interdependent, where the boundaries between oneself and others are less distinct (Markus & Kitayama, 1991). This sense of self is based on the fundamental interconnectedness among people.

Another dimension extremely important to understanding cultural differences in emotion is Status Differentiation (SD—Matsumoto, 1991). This dimension refers to the degree to which cultures will maintain status differences among its members. High SD cultures provide institutions, mores, and rules to maintain status differences; low SD cultures minimize such differences. This dimension is conceptually related to Hofstede's (1980, 1983) dimension known as Power Distance (PD; also discussed by Mulder, 1976, 1977). According to Hofstede, PD refers to the degree to which cultures maintain power differences among their members. I prefer the SD distinction because I believe that cultures use status, through position, title, or place, as a vehicle by which they either maintain or minimize differences in power. That is, cultures will differ in the degree to which they influence their members' attributions of power to status. Also, the PD dimension confuses the concepts of power and status, whereas the focus of SD is clearly on power afforded to status.

These two dimensions of culture, IC and SD, are certainly relevant to the Japanese culture, and the discussion of them in relation to the Japanese culture is not new. Many authors have pointed out that the Japanese culture is much more group-oriented than Western cultures, and that individualism in Japan is sacrificed for the sake of the group. These kinds of discussions focus on the collectivist aspect of IC, and characterize Japanese culture basically as a collectivist one. Some writers (e.g., Nakane, 1970) have also suggested that vertical status relationships are an integral part of the Japanese culture. These notions also speak to the relatively high degree of status differentiation in the Japanese culture.

For the most part, writers in the past have focused generally either on the collective nature of the Japanese culture or on its high status differentiation, and not on the joint influences of both dimensions on the individual Japanese. But the Japanese culture is not made up of any one, single dimension of culture that can characterize all possible cultural influences. A more accurate picture of the Japanese culture must incorporate at least these two dimensions of variability simultaneously, and even then, there will undoubtedly be aspects of group and individual behavior that are not accounted for by IC and SD. In this case, we need to continue our search for other meaningful and relevant dimensions of cultural variability that can account for variability among people not accounted for by IC and SD. By utilizing both concepts of IC and SD as global concepts related to culture, we can not only examine the Japanese culture itself but also place Japan within a larger global perspective.

Take, as an example, Hofstede's (1980, 1983) large-scale, multinational study of work-related values. This study was probably the first to examine differences on these dimensions across a wide range of cultures. Surveying over 50 different countries, Hofstede rank-ordered each of them according to the degree to which their respondents harbored or endorsed values related to IC or SD. On SD (which was studied as Power Distance in his research), for instance, Japan was ranked above the United States, pointing out the relative importance of SD to the Japanese culture. This is consistent with our anecdotal impression of the Japanese culture and with previous discussions of it (e.g., Nakane, 1970). However, Japan was ranked quite low on the scale, at 21, and the United States at 25, only four points lower. Countries such as the Philippines, Mexico, and Venezuela were rated much higher than Japan on the SD scale, and countries such as Denmark, Israel, and Austria were even lower than the United States.

The same differentials were true for IC. In Hofstede's (1980, 1983) study, the U.S. scored no. 1 on IC, pointing out the individualistic nature of the American culture. Japan was rated no. 22. This difference corresponds quite nicely with previous works expounding individual vs. group differences between the U.S. and Japan. But on the scale of 50, Pakistan, Colombia, and Venezuela were the lowest, suggesting that they are even more collectivist than Japan.

Thus, it is not necessarily true that IC and SD represent "new" dimensions by which to understand the Japanese culture. They certainly have been discussed by previous Japan scholars as well. But IC and SD do at least represent meaningful, pancultural dimensions of variability that can be used to understand cultural differences across many different nations, not limited to anecdotal or impressionistic differences. It is precisely this type of global perspective that a dimensional approach provides, and that we have adopted, in our cross-cultural research program.

Other pancultural dimensions of culture have been suggested in addition to IC and SD. Hofstede (1980, 1983), for example, suggests at least two others. Uncertainty Avoidance (UA), which refers to the institutions and rituals that cultures have developed in order to deal with the anxiety relating to uncertainty; and Masculinity-Femininity (MA), which refers to the degree to which cultures foster gender differences among their members. Pelto (1968) suggested that cultures could be thought of as either "loose" or "tight," according to the degree of homogeneity that existed within them. The incorporation of these other meaningful dimensions of cultural variability will allow us to examine the influences of the Japanese culture above and beyond those that can be accounted for by IC and SD. The MA dimension, for example, is useful to describe the degree to which the Japanese culture fosters gender differences among its members. In Hofstede's (1980) study, Japan scored highest on MA, implicating the importance of this dimension to an understanding of the Japanese culture. UA is also important in understanding many of the ritualistic types of behaviors (festivals, religions, etc.) that the Japanese culture has developed to deal with anxiety concerning the future. These ritualistic activities play a major role in maintaining the tradition of the Japanese culture and heritage over generations.

In addition, the incorporation of dimensions such as MA, UA, and others, in future research paradigms will make it possible for comparisons and studies on Japan to be conducted within a global perspective, using the same dimensions to describe similar tendencies in many different cultures around the world. By studying one country, say Japan, within a global context, we can improve our research within a single culture.

In our work, we have focused solely on IC and SD, not because we suggest no other dimensions to be important but because IC and SD are so large and robust that it will be years before research can explore their possibilities and move on to other avenues. For our purposes, the remainder of the discussion in this chapter will focus on these two dimensions. It is my hope that other research programs pick up on other relevant cultural dimensions such as MA and UA, and investigate thoroughly their contributions to similarities and differences on emotion.

Understanding Emotions in Japan as a Function of IC and SD

Many of the recent studies we have conducted in Japan on human emotion have forced us to think hard about just how and why Japanese cultural similarities and differences occur. There was no previous theoretical model of cultural influences on emotion to fall back on because there had been no attempt, until recently, to offer a cross-cultural theory of emotional expression or perception. It is true that the neurocultural theory of emotional expression presented in Chapter 3 did exist, but scientists interested in emotions across cultures for a long time erroneously assumed that the neurocultural theory is a cross-cultural theory of emotion, whereas it is really a theory of expression mechanics—that is, it tells us how cultural similarities and differences can occur, but it does not reveal the exact nature of cultures and cultural differences or why cultural differences exist. We do not know what it is about the Japanese culture that produces the cultural display and decoding rules boxes that result in a distinctive culture.

A few years ago my laboratory began to take a close look at this most difficult question. What became clear quite quickly is that most cross-cultural studies of emotion did not have a good definition of culture itself. All the cross-cultural studies of emotion conducted to date, my own included, have defined culture by country. For example, studies of American and Japanese cultural differences on emotion have used samples from the United States and Japan. Likewise, all other cross-cultural research has used samples from *countries*. Researchers have proceeded on the assumption that culture is a unique phenomenon for each country, so that a sample of respondents from the United States would represent the American culture, a sample of respondents from Japan would represent the Japanese culture, and so on. In fact, there is another level of assumption at work in such assumptions—that is, that we know what the American and Japanese cultures are in the first place.

Moreover, the samples in most cross-cultural research are really not from a country; they are from cities within countries, and they do not usually represent the entire city but are recruited from a university that happens to be in that city. Further, respondents are not randomly selected within universities; they are recruited from specific courses within specific departments, such as introductory psychology (here in the United States) or in courses taught by collaborating researchers. Thus, our cross-cultural studies are really cross-university or cross-course studies in their most limited sense.

Undoubtedly, there are considerable and meaningful cultural differences that underlie these less-than-random samples, and we must grant that the assumptions that researchers have made in the past are not without some merit. Nonetheless, the practice of recruiting university students from a course in a university in a city in a country to exemplify culture has not been challenged in relation to the question of how we conceptualize culture theoretically, and how that theoretical concept is at work in our research. Consequently, although many of these studies are surely cross-cultural, they are sorely lacking in the sense that cultural differences, when found, are often interpreted in terms of stereotype, anecdote, or impression, rather than on the basis of some meaningful, theoretical dimensions of culture. In fact, there is no other alternative than to make these assumptions about underlying culture without the existence of an objective way to measure culture reliably on the individual level.

Cross-cultural research can only truly advance if we consider how countries differ on stable and meaningful dimensions of cultural variability. If these types of theoretical dimensions can be found, then we can use these to interpret the cultural differences that we find in our research, instead of relying on stereotypical or anecdotal impressions. This philosophy therefore forces us to search the social psychological, sociological, and anthropological literatures for these kinds of dimensions. This search led us to realize the importance of IC and SD in understanding cultures.

Just deciding which dimensions are important was, however, only the beginning of our task. The next, more important, task was to develop a theoretical framework with which we could understand, and predict, how IC and SD would produce differences in Japanese emotional expressions, and why. Our efforts fell short because we realized that a direct link between IC and SD as macrocultural constructs cannot be made with emotion as an individual, personal construct. There was a missing link in the components of a cultural framework of emotion that prevented us from developing such a theoretical framework. To address this link, we utilized the sociological distinctions known as Ingroups and Outgroups.

IC INFLUENCES ON EMOTION IN JAPAN AS A FUNCTION OF INGROUPS AND OUTGROUPS

Some general theoretical concepts. The ingroups-outgroup distinction is one of the most basic distinctions in social psychology and sociology (see Brewer & Kramer, 1985; Messick & Mackie, 1989; Tajfel, 1982, for reviews). The familiarity and intimacy of self-ingroup relations provide the safety and comfort to express emotions freely and to tolerate a broader spectrum of emotional behaviors. Self-outgroup relationships lack this flexibility and tolerance. For example, people generally feel more comfortable in expressing emotions to their families than to strangers in public. The familiarity, intimacy, and previous history of tolerance in the family provides a context where emotions may be expressed that does not exist with strangers. Part of emotion socialization involves the learning of just who the ingroup and outgroup members are and the appropriate behaviors associated with them.

Of course, there may be variations to this consistency. Some families, for example, may allow for the expression of certain emotions but not others. Some people may express emotions in public the way they do in familiar quarters. Drawing lines of appropriate and inappropriate contexts must serve to describe the modal scenario of display rules, while fully acknowledging the existence of sometimes considerable individual, family, or subcultural differences to the mode.

With the ingroup-outgroup distinction, we could consider how IC differences in culture would interact with ingroups and outgroups to produce differences in emotional expressions. Cultural differences in the *meanings* of self-ingroup and self-outgroup relationships (see Triandis, Bontempo, Villareal, Asai, & Lucca, 1988) produce cultural differences in emotional behavior. Individualistic cultures have more ingroups, and their members are not attached to any single ingroup because there are numerous ingroups to which they can be attached. The survival of societies in individualistic cultures depends to a large degree upon the efficiency of the individual members rather than on their ingroups. The survival of societies in collectivist cultures depends much more on the effective functioning of groups rather than individuals, and their commitment to ingroups is greater than in individualistic cultures.

Thus, self-ingroup relationships differ in individualistic and collectivist cultures in the degree of harmony, cohesion, cooperation, and conformity between the self and others. Collectivist cultures foster a greater degree of conformity within their ingroups, and sanctions exist for nonconformity. A high degree of conformity ensures that the individual is identified and bonded with his or her ingroup, thus allowing groups to function smoothly. Surrendering personal goals in favor of collective ones is a necessity of collectivism. Individualistic cultures foster less conformity within groups because identification with groups and the effective functioning of its groups are not crucial to the culture's survival.

Self-outgroup relationships are also different in individualistic and collectivist cultures. Collectivist cultures emphasize greater distinctions toward outgroups because of the greater degree of harmony required in the ingroups. In individualistic cultures, this difference is not as clear. Self-outgroup relationships do not differ from self-ingroup as much, and members of individualistic cultures will not distinguish, or discriminate against, outgroup members as readily as will members of collectivist cultures.

Using this theoretical framework, I suggested elsewhere (Matsumoto, 1990, 1991) that cultural differences on IC would produce differences in the display of emotion as a function of ingroups and outgroups. In comparison with individualistic cultures, members of collectivist cultures should display more positive emotions to ingroups, because of the culture's greater pressure to maintain harmony within the ingroups. At the same time, they should display more negative emotions to outgroups. This would serve to maintain and reinforce the distinctions between ingroups and outgroups, a distinction that is much more important to maintain in collectivist cultures than in individualistic cultures.

Conversely, members of individualistic cultures should display more negative emotions to ingroups. It is easier to express negative emotions within ingroups in individualistic cultures because of the relatively smaller degree of commitment, attachment, and need of people of individualistic cultures to maintain harmony and cohesion within ingroups. Also, members of individualistic cultures should display more positive emotions to outgroups, because there is relatively less pressure to maintain distinctions between ingroups and outgroups. Indeed, individualistic cultures will tend to view people in general as equal to themselves (Figure 7).

IC in Japan. These ideas are well suited to understanding cultural similarities and differences in the emotions of the Japanese. Of

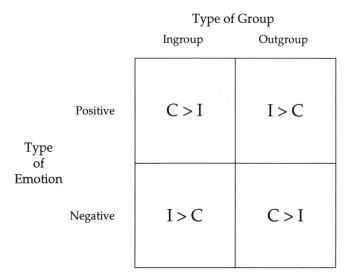

Fig. 7. Individualism-Collectivism, Ingroups-Outgroups, and Emotional Expression Predictions. I = Individualistic Culture (e.g., U.S.A.), C = Collective Culture (e.g., Japan).

course, the existence of ingroups and outgroups is not unique to Japan; they are universal social distinctions that exist in all cultures because they emerge from any type of system where the formation of groups is necessary for the survival of the individual members. What makes the Japanese culture special and different is not the fact that ingroups, outgroups, and status differences exist; rather, it is the particular rules, attitudes, and shared behaviors the Japanese foster about ingroups and outgroups that make the culture unique.

The rules of the Japanese culture center around the fostering of collectivist values and behaviors; the Japanese culture fosters the importance of groups much more than it fosters the importance of individuals—almost to the total exclusion of individualistic needs or desires. Because of the collective nature of the Japanese culture, ingroups are the chief social frame of conduct: one's ingroup is a major part of one's life, and its influences on one's behavior are pervasive. As a result, a major part of consciousness is taken up by considerations of one's ingroup. Japanese culture not only fosters but demands that individuals make sacrifices for the group.

The collective nature of the Japanese culture in relation to ingroups and outgroups produces severe demands on interpersonal relationships as well. Within ingroups in Japan, concepts such as harmony, cohesion, cooperation, conformity, and tightness are extremely important. The Japanese culture is structured to ensure the maintenance of harmonious relationships among its ingroup members, to ensure the cohesion of the group, and to facilitate cooperation among its group members in order to ensure the survival of the group, and therefore also of the persons who constitute that group.

In addition to harmony, concepts related to individual humility are extremely important in Japan. Exhibiting humility in Japan is to be humble, and maintaining one's humility means that one maintains one's unchanging standing with the rest of one's ingroup. To accept individual recognition is a sign of arrogance, and makes one stand out. Standing out in Japan threatens group cohesion, because in standing out emphasis is placed on individuals not groups. In Japan, phrases such as "The nail that sticks out will be pounded down" reflect the attitude of the Japanese culture, which is necessary because of its collectivist nature.

Of course, it stands to reason that Japanese are ultrasensitive toward what others will think of them. They focus exclusively on how others (i.e., the "group") will interpret their decisions or actions. Transgression of socially appropriate standards and rules brings out shame and ridicule. The extreme concern for other's opinions about one's own behavior and the influence it wields in determining to a large degree the outcomes provide the vehicle by which shame can be used as an agent of social control.

Japan's collectivist culture also has ramifications for outgroups. Anything or anyone that is outside one's group is peripheral to one's existence. Competition among groups can be particularly fierce, not only in the field of sports but also in business. The baseball rivalry between Waseda and Keio universities, though more openly displayed, is no less intense than the rivalry between, say, Matsushita and Panasonic, or between Kobe Steel and Asahi Steel, and it results from the same "us vs. them" mentality of the ingroup animosity toward outgroups. Competitions between groups in Japan have a life of their own because of the collective nature of the Japanese culture and the requirements it imposes on group behavior. Fierce competition and ritual loyalty serve to maintain, and foster, ingroup cohesion and harmony.

The pervasiveness of the importance in Japanese culture of collectivism and its effects on ingroups and outgroups can be seen in the Japanese attitudes toward anything new or foreign. Anything that is new or foreign, whether it be material goods or people of different races, countries, or citizenship, is often considered an outgroup manifestation. Witness, for example, the problems that have occurred in recent years because of Japanese political leaders' remarks concerning non-Asian minorities in the United States. This sort of xenophobia is fostered by the culture not only in terms of other people, but of anything that can be considered outgroup to oneself.

In the United States, where there is much less emphasis on the group and much greater emphasis on individuality, the average person is not required to make continuing sacrifices for group needs, and one's identity as an individual American is not as determined by group membership. There is less emphasis on harmony or cohesion within ingroups, because there are fewer bonds to the ingroups, and there are also more ingroups to which one can belong, and can enter and leave at will.

Individualistic cultures thus produce different requirements in terms of interpersonal relationships within groups. There is less need to maintain harmony, and less necessity to be always conscious of others. To the extent that social control agents can be imposed, guilt rather than shame becomes the primary social control agent. Shame implies a comparison of one's individual behavior against the standards imposed by others; guilt does not carry the same social implications, and it is therefore less salient in collectivist cultures and more salient in individualistic cultures. Members of individualistic cultures such as that of the United States are freer to interact with other individuals and groups without regard to group membership, interpersonal harmony, or concern for the opinions of others.

SD INFLUENCES ON EMOTIONS IN JAPAN

Some general theoretical issues. As discussed earlier, SD is another important dimension to consider in our theorizing about cultural differences on emotion, in Japan as well as cross-culturally. Status differences are found in all cultures, and all cultures will differ in the degree to which they foster the maintenance or minimizing of those status differences.

In comparison with low-SD cultures, members of high-SD cul-

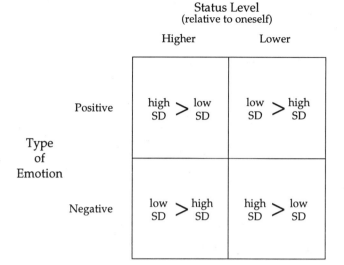

Fig. 8. Emotion Differences as a Function of Status and Cultural Differences in Status Differentiation. High SD = high status Differentiating Culture (e.g., Japan); low SD = low status Differentiating Culture (e.g., U.S.A.)

tures should display more positive emotions to higher-status others, and more negative emotions to lower-status others. The display of positive emotions to higher-status others should serve as signals of appeasement and deference. On the other hand, the display of negative emotions to lower-status others should serve to maintain one's own higher status. Conversely, members of low-SD cultures should display more negative emotions to higher-status others, and more positive emotions to lower-status others. The display of negative emotions toward higher-status others would be more tolerated in low-SD cultures because these cultures are less inclined to maintain status differences. The display of positive emotions to lower-status others would also be congruent with the minimizing of status differences across people. The theoretical assumption underlying these hypotheses is that violation of any of these rules would threaten the degree of status differentiation that exists in status relationships (see Figure 8).

SD in Japan. Japan is clearly no exception to cultural differences on SD, being one of the strongest cultures in the world where status differences are maintained. This cultural dimension is directly related to the well-known notion of Japan as a vertical society (Nakane, 1970). The Japanese culture fosters differentiation according to status, and it has many rules and social institutions to maintain status differences. Transgression of these rules threatens the status relationships that exist between interactants, and thus is contrary to the Japanese culture.

One manifestation of the high degree of status differentiation in the Japanese culture can be seen in the terms of address used in the Japanese language (Suzuki, 1973). These terms of address are completely determined by one's role, position, or status. For example, a teacher is always called *sensei* (teacher), and never by his or her first name. Bosses are called according to their position (e.g., section chief, president), and not by their name. People lower than oneself in status, however, can be called by their names, and suffixes can be added to make it clear that they are subordinate.

The Japanese culture is structured in such a way that lower status always defers to higher status, regardless of how status is defined. In many instances, status can be defined by age, so that younger always defers to older. Even among twins, the child that is born first is called the "older brother" or "older sister," allowing for status differentiation between them. In other instances, status can be defined by rank, so that lower rank defers to higher rank. Most often, Japanese social institutions are structured in such a way that age and rank increase simultaneously. Consider, for example, the ways by which Japanese workers move up the ladder in business environments. Regardless of how brilliant one was as a student, when one enters the company one is placed at the bottom of the totem pole. Whatever one's abilities, one often has to endure the stress of having been relegated to menial and meaningless jobs. As time passes, people can work their way up the corporate ladder, but only if they are "Japanese" enough—that is, if they truly subordinate any private life and circumscribe their existence around their company, and if they have tolerated the status differentiation that needs to be maintained. The length of time this system has been in effect ensures that it is here to stay for a while, at least. In recent years there seems to be an increasing trend in the direction of recognizing exceptional abilities in the form of benefits and rewards, but the system is still far more rigid than systems in the United States that are considerably less status differentiating.

In Japan, it is easy to interpret who is higher or lower in status when you see people in a group interact. Everything revolves around the status differences, including the vocabulary, terms of address, posture, gestures, and facial expressions. When two people bow to each other, the status differential that exists between them is obvious, because the person who is the lower in status will usually bow lower.

Consider again the United States in relation to status differentiation. Although the American culture also fosters status differentiation to some degree, it is clearly not as strong or pervasive as that in the Japanese culture. In the United States, status lines are often blurred. Relations between teachers and students are often casual, not formal, and to a certain degree, at least up to the higher echelons, workers and bosses treat each other as equals. There is no special language to address superiors or subordinates; for the most part, "I" and "you" work very well. Age, too, has less meaning in the United States than in Japan, and climbing the corporate ladder in the U.S. is more dependent upon individual ability than on seniority. All these differences are due to the fact that the U.S. places less emphasis on status differentiation, and Americans are freer to engage in behaviors that threaten, or disregard, status differences between interactants. The social system, which regards individual ability, plays a large role in maintaining this culture.

EMPIRICAL SUPPORT FOR THESE IDEAS

A study presented earlier in Chapter 3 on display rules supports many of these ideas concerning IC and SD influences on emotions in Japan. Without repeating the study in detail, I highlight some particular aspects in order to recast some of the interpretations of the findings in light of the discussion in this chapter on IC and SD influences on emotions.

American and Japanese participants were asked how appropriate they thought it would be to express six of the universal emotions (anger, disgust, fear, happiness, sadness, and surprise) in eight different social situations (alone, with family, with friends, with casual acquaintances, in public, with people of lower status than oneself, with people of higher status than oneself, and with children). The analyses revealed important cultural differences. For example, the Americans rated disgust and sadness more acceptable with close friends and family members, whereas the Japanese rated anger and fear more appropriate with casual acquaintances and in public. The Japanese also rated anger more appropriate than the Americans with people of lower status, and fear more appropriate with people of higher status. Finally, the Americans rated disgust and sadness more acceptable with children than did the Japanese.

This pattern of findings is entirely consistent with the concepts described in this chapter involving IC and SD. The Americans rated disgust and sadness more appropriate with close friends and family members because individualistic cultures tolerate the display of negative emotions to ingroup others more than the collectivist Japanese culture. The Japanese rated anger and fear more appropriate with acquaintances and the public because the collectivist Japanese culture needs to differentiate more between ingroups and outgroups, allowing for the expression of negative emotions to outgroups. The Japanese rated anger more appropriate with people of lower status than did the Americans, because the status-differentiating Japanese culture requires the maintenance of status differences more than the American culture. Likewise, the Japanese rated fear more appropriate with people of higher status because of deference. One can see clearly how each of these findings can be accounted for in the predictions made in Figures 7 and 8.

As described earlier in this chapter, one chief advantage to understanding and studying cultural differences using a dimensional approach (such as IC and SD) is that we are able to test the same ideas in other cultures. This ability provides us with a valuable perspective that is unattainable with previous, culture-specific approaches to hypothesis testing. Other cultures also vary on dimensions such as IC and SD. By testing the model presented in Figures 7 and 8 in other cultures, we can examine directly the degree to which the theoretical model gains support as a general conceptual framework for understanding emotions in many different cultures, not just the Japanese.

In one study, we did exactly that (Matsumoto & Hearn, 1991). This study, using exactly the same methodology as the one described immediately above, involved respondents from the United States, Poland, and Hungary. The Polish and Hungarian cultures are considerably more collectivist than the American culture (Triandis, 1992), thus providing another test of these ideas. In this study, Americans rated negative emotions in ingroups more appropriate than did Poles and Hungarians, Poles and Hungarians rated positive emotions in ingroups more appropriate than Americans, and they also rated negative emotions in outgroups more appropriate than Americans. Thus, the data from this study also correspond almost exactly with the theoretical predictions made in Figure 7, and correspond very well with the data obtained in Japan.

In addition to these two studies, we have also conducted several studies examining cultural differences in emotion judgments as a function of IC differences (Matsumoto, 1989a, 1992a). In one of these (Matsumoto, 1989a), the percent of agreement in emotion labeling across the cultures sampled in Ekman and Izard's original universality studies was correlated with Hofstede's IC and SD scores for these countries. Correlations were found for several of the emotions, suggesting how cultural differences in IC and SD can influence the judgment of emotion. The correlations, moreover, were all the more impressive in that the data that were correlated came from different studies, conducted by different researchers at different times.

The studies reported earlier in Chapter 5 on the ecology of emotion-eliciting events of the Japanese also support this model. For example, joy occurred very rarely inside unfamiliar places in Japan compared with the United States and Europe. Also, the Japanese were much more likely than Americans and Europeans to experience sadness inside unfamiliar settings and outside. The Japanese also reported more fear and anger outside and in unfamiliar places; because those most likely refer to outgroup situations, this finding seems entirely predictable according to Figure 7. In addition, the Japanese reported less fear inside familiar places, which also corresponds with our predictions concerning ingroups.

Further correspondence emerged in analyzing the data reported in Chapter 5 that the emotions for most respondents occurred when they were alone, in a dyad, or in a small group. Across the board, the Japanese experienced more emotions in dyads than did the Americans and the Europeans, and significantly fewer emotions alone. The Japanese tended to report a significantly greater percentage of events involving familiar people than did the Americans or Europeans. These findings also speak to the separation of emotion according to social situation, and cultural differences on this separation according to IC.

Studies conducted by other researchers also point to the connection between IC and emotion. Gudykunst and Ting-Toomey (1988), for example, correlated data from Scherer and Wallbott's large, cross-cultural study of emotion antecedents (Wallbott & Scherer, 1986) with Hofstede's (1980) country scores on IC and three other dimensions. They found a number of interesting correlations between IC score differences and emotion antecedents. Wallbott and Scherer (1988) correlated self-reported emotion variables obtained in their cross-cultural research program with Gross National Product (GNP) levels, which they theorized to be correlated with IC differences. These researchers also found substantial correlations between IC (via GNP) and self-reported emotional reactions.

Thus, there is considerable support for the theoretical ideas summarized in Figures 7 and 8. More importantly, these ideas, and these studies, are significant not only for what they tell us about Japan but also in terms of how we can understand Japanese cultural similarities and differences in relation to other cultures. The use of pancultural dimensions of variability like IC and SD affords us this possibility.

IC AND SD INFLUENCES ON JAPANESE DISPLAY RULES

In Chapter 3 I described some speculative hypotheses about Japanese display rules. Again, there is no need to be redundant here by going into them in great detail, but I mention them very briefly to illustrate their relevance to IC and SD. They are directly related to IC and SD because they either (1) maintain harmony and cohesion within ingroups, and to differentiate outgroups; or (2) maintain status differences among high-, low-, and same-status others.

The importance of collective emotion. The sharing of emotional expressions and experiences strengthens bonds among group members, thereby filling an important role in group functioning. Individual emotional expressions must conform to the group emotion; if they do not, then group harmony and solidarity are threatened and social sanctions such as shame, ridicule, or isolation may follow. The sharing of collective emotion is an important display rule in Japan that is closely tied to IC. The sharing of emotions serves to maintain the Japanese culture's collective orientation.

The maintenance of group harmony. When interacting with other members of their group, the Japanese must take particular care to ensure that the harmony of the group is not threatened by dangerous emotions and that peace exists. This is also related to IC. As we have seen, the preservation of group harmony, peace, and cohesion is especially important in collective cultures such as Japan.

Ingroup and outgroup differentiation. In Japan, it is important to differentiate between one's ingroup and other outgroups by displaying outright indifference or even anger and disgust toward members of other groups, even solely on the basis of group membership. This serves to differentiate us from them—that is, to differentiate one's own group from others, thereby further strengthening group bonds and fostering group rivalry. Again, this is directly related to IC; people of collectivist cultures such as Japan's need to differentiate ingroups from outgroups to a much greater degree than do members of individualistic cultures such as the U.S.

The importance of future relationships. If the Japanese believe that there is a possibility for future, harmonious relations with someone else, then they must express emotion in such a way as not to threaten this future harmony. If the Japanese believe that there is no possibility of such future relationships, then there is no need to try to establish or maintain interpersonal harmony. This differential is also directly related to IC and the preservation of ingroup harmony in collectivistic cultures like Japan.

Deference to higher-status others. If someone is of higher status than oneself, then one must display emotions so as to reinforce an awareness of the difference in status. This is directly related to the Japanese culture's propensity toward high status differentiation.

The maintenance of one's own high status. Higher-status persons in Japan must also behave in ways that maintain status differentials. For example, it is definitely more acceptable for a higher-status person to show anger to lower-status others than vice versa. The ability of a higher-status person to display anger toward lower-status others maintains, if not enlarges, status differences, especially if those of a lower status do not have the same privilege. Again, this is directly related to the Japanese culture's propensity toward high status differentiation.

IC, SD, and the Japanese Culture

Both IC and SD are very powerful concepts that can be used to understand cultures and to make predictions about cultural similarities and differences in emotional behaviors. These concepts are powerful because they are pancultural: all cultures around the world must deal with matters concerning individuals vs. groups, and status differences. These dimensions are also meaningful in that they account for a major portion of any culture's influence on the behavior of its members. And because they are dimensions that are not based in race, ethnicity, or nationality, they offer new and exciting ways of defining cultures as a social-psychological construct.

To be sure, these dimensions have been discussed quite often with regard to Japan. Many students of Japanese culture have pointed out the group orientation of the Japanese culture, and the subordination of the individual to the group. Many scholars have also pointed out the vertical nature of status relationships in Japan. But the material presented here is a departure in that it takes both concepts, IC and SD, and treats them as equally important dimensions of culture that influence individual behavior, emotions, thoughts, and feelings, of the Japanese society. The present work does not choose one or the other of these dimensions; rather, I believe that the power of these dimensions is that their dual influence on the feelings and emotions of the Japanese must be examined in order to understand those emotions better.

The material presented here gives us a way not only of understanding the Japanese culture and people but also of placing Japan in a larger, more global perspective. Because IC and SD are universally important dimensions, our attempts to define the Japanese culture and people according to these dimensions can incorporate similar attempts with other people and other cultures. As explained earlier, this global approach to understanding cultures and people is sorely needed even now in this increasingly pluralistic world, and will be an even greater necessity in future years.

This approach is not without certain drawbacks, however. Its major limitation has to do with the meaning of culture itself. Certainly, no culture can be reduced to a two-dimensional concept. Culture is a rich and complex blend of history, principles of government, manners, customs, religions, music, art, architecture, and so on. It is obvious that there is much more to any culture, including the Japanese, than simply a classification as individualistic or collective, and high or low status differentiating. Unfortunately, our attempt to classify cultures in relation to the IC and SD is only a feeble effort toward capturing that global, amorphous mass that we know as the Japanese culture. That understood, we must try to see exactly how much about the emotions of the Japanese we can explain with these concepts. Certainly, there will be some things that we simply cannot explain with these concepts. At that point, our next job will be to search for other dimensions or aspects of culture that will explain those aspects of emotion that IC and SD do not.

It is left to future research to investigate many of these concerns. We must try ourselves to develop new ways of looking at culture by means of IC and SD, though at the same time being cognizant of what IC and SD cannot accomplish. When the dust settles, however, my bet is that these two dimensions of culture will account for quite a lot of emotional behavior of the Japanese, and we will come to the conclusion that IC and SD are quite robust.

Chapter 9

Conclusion

As our conceptual understanding of the Japanese culture, and its impact on emotion, improves, we face a future that will surely test that understanding and our ability to use it in both research and applied settings. This final chapter presents some ideas concerning what I believe are the most relevant issues for research and practical use. Below I outline five issues for research and four for practice that emerge from the ideas discussed in this book so far. These are only outlines of ideas, and other issues not mentioned below deserve attention in both science and application. Some of these were mentioned throughout the text. While not minimizing the importance of these other issues, the following ideas are offered as guidelines for some of our efforts in the future.

A Research Agenda for Emotions in Japan

DISPLAY RULES

Display rules are one of the most important concepts in cross-cultural psychology and offer academicians and laypersons alike a measure for judging a wide range of phenomena. Although cross-cultural studies on display rules have focused on Japan, there is still much more to do. What we need is a survey of display rules, across genders, classes, and ages in Japan, that assesses what these rules may be for the various emotions. Although the recent studies have taken a few steps in this direction, we sorely need to get even more of this basic information concerning display rules in Japan. Other potential avenues of research include studies of the degree to which Japanese display rules are associated with other psychological or sociological characteristics, such as place of living, age, socioeconomic status, and occupation.

SECONDARY EMOTIONS

Secondary emotions are emotional reactions to emotions, and as mentioned earlier, they are an important part of the emotional life of the individual Japanese. In suppressing anger toward a superior, for example, a person may have a variety of secondary emotional reactions, ranging from even more intense anger to acceptance and depression. Because of the Japanese culture's emphasis on the modification of overt emotional displays according to social circumstances, secondary emotional reactions play a much larger role in the Japanese culture, and have greater meaning to the individual Japanese than they do in Western cultures such as that of the United States.

In spite of their importance, secondary emotions have not received any attention in the scientific literature. One reason for this, I believe, concerns the dominance of Western research practices in the scientific literature. Because secondary emotions are less important in Western culture, they receive less consideration by Western researchers, and do not find priority in active research. Most Americans, academics and laypeople alike, take the attitude that the emotion that is expressed is all the emotion that is being felt. Indeed, this perception about emotions underlies most American and Western psychological theories about emotion, and these theories, in turn, drive most research on emotion. Even research on emotions conducted in Japan is influenced heavily by American and Western theories (cf. Matsumoto, Kudoh, & Takeuchi, 1995), compounding the problem.

Ironically, it is not the case that these ideas have never been offered in Western psychology. Such influential emotion theorists as Sylvan Tomkins, usually acknowledged as the father of current scientific interest in emotion, and Carrol Izard have discussed concepts of emotion that are very close to the idea of secondary emotions as presented in this book. Tomkins (1984), for example, offers the notion of "backed-up affect," which, though not identical to my ideas about secondary emotions, is similar in the sense that it adds another layer of complexity to the emotion process. These ideas have not enjoyed the attention of researchers to the same degree as other, more "obvious" aspects of emotion, however, at least in scientific approaches to date. With the recognition of the importance of secondary emotional reactions to understanding human emotions across cultures, perhaps researchers will begin to expand their studies to include this important aspect of emotion.

THE STUDY OF DECEPTION

The study of the ability to deceive, and to detect deception, is intrinsically fascinating to most people. To date, most of the knowledge that has been generated in the literature on deception has originated from research laboratories interested in human emotion and nonverbal behavior (e.g., see Ekman, 1985). Emotion is an especially relevant topic for a couple of reasons. First, emotions can be the focus of a lie, as when people lie about their emotions (e.g., saying that they are feeling happy when they are actually miserable). Second, even when emotions are not the direct focus of a lie, they are inevitably intertwined with the deception process, because people may fear being caught or feel guilty about lying, and so forth.

To the extent that cultural display rules dictate a modification of overt behavior from what one truly feels, they can themselves be thought of as a cultural mechanism for deception. This means that cultures such as the Japanese culture that, because of display rules, require members to modify their behavior depending on social circumstances will foster a relatively better ability to deceive others, and perhaps also to detect deception in others. This is an area that may well receive more attention owing to our increased recognition of the effects of cultural display rules in Japan and an improved awareness of the relationship between display rules and emotion.

EMOTIONS AND HEALTH

Researchers, practitioners, and the lay public alike in the U.S. have all come to realize the important relationship between emotions and health. Currently, massive information dissemination efforts have educated many Americans about the links between stress and cancer, anger and Type A behavior with cardiovascular disease, emotional volatility and diabetes, and so on. These effects have been congruent with increased funding and research on these areas bridging psychology and medicine over the past two decades, and reflect areas of even greater investigation in the years to come.

Certainly in Japan the relationship between emotions and physical health is an area ripe for study. On one hand, the relatively severe cultural influences under which the Japanese must exist, particularly insofar as they demand the suppression of toxic, negative emotions, might suggest severe adverse effects on health. Yet some studies have documented a lower incidence of illnesses such as cardiovascular diseases in the Japanese population, compared with Americans, which would tend not to support such claims (Marmot & Syme, 1976; Triandis et al., 1988). These types of opposing viewpoints and observations lend themselves to an area primed for research, and could lead to many other branches of study related to health outcomes. For example, could cultural differences in diet offset to a large degree the negative effects of emotions on health in Japan? Or, are there other social outlets in Japan that allow for the dissipation of the negative effects of emotion control, such as after-hours carousing and socializing? Triandis et al. (1988) suggest that greater emphasis on collective behavior results in stronger social support networks that buffer against cardiovascular risk factors. Do these outlets themselves lead to other negative health outcomes that are not as prevalent in the U.S. (e.g., alcoholism)?

Questions such as these represent important areas of research and study in the future that find their roots in basic cross-cultural research on display rules and emotions. With the expertise that we have developed studying these same phenomena in the United States, we are in a very good position to break into this important line of study in Japan as well.

JAPANESE CULTURE IN THE INDIVIDUAL JAPANESE

A more careful definition of what we mean by "culture" is an important matter facing all cross-cultural researchers today. The dimensional approach to understanding cultures, highlighted in the last chapter by IC and SD, affords many unique possibilities and advantages over traditional approaches to understanding culture via country labels, at least in psychological research. Still, we need to take that approach even further if we are to improve our understanding of the influence of culture on individual emotions. Although most people think of culture as a macrolevel, social construct, culture is at the same time a highly personal, individual construct. In one sense, culture can be defined by the degree to which a group of people shares norms, attitudes, values, or behavior, but I believe that that definition of culture exists to different degrees in different individuals. For example, while any two people may be of the same general culture, one may truly be steeped in that culture, reflecting in his or her behavior the norm that exists in his or her group. The other, however, may manifest that culture to a much lesser degree, exhibiting behavior or harboring beliefs that are not entirely consistent with the group norm.

What is truly needed in research is a way to measure culture, or a dimension of it (e.g., IC, SD), in individuals. If we can find such a way, we will no longer have to assume that our samples in our studies are different on the relevant cultural variables; instead, we can measure them and quantify that difference. Different degrees of group cultural similarities and differences may be related to the degree to which the samples in the study differed on the relevant cultural variables. Moreover, these scores can be used as covariates in group difference analyses, adding statistical power to the research paradigm, in addition to the added conceptual power.

This is a practice that is much needed in cross-cultural work. To give an example, are we to accept the estimates of some (e.g., Triandis, 1992) that even within the Japanese culture, 30 percent of the Japanese surveyed appear to harbor individualistic attitudes and values, rather than the collectivist values traditionally thought to characterize all Japanese? Without psychometrically sound ways of measuring the relevant dimensions of culture on the level of the individual, we cannot be sure of the validity of cross-cultural research on the emotions.

At the time of this writing, several measures of IC have been developed by different research teams around the world, including our own laboratory (see Matsumoto, Weissman, Preston, & Brown, 1993). Future research attempts to use these types of measures in the cross-cultural study of emotion will be a major plus for cross-cultural research, and for our understanding of Japanese emotions.

Integrating Research with Practice

In today's multicultural and pluralistic world, where cross-racial, -national, and -cultural interactions are frequent in personal and professional life, considerations of cultural differences in emotional experience, expression, and perception are increasingly important. Research on these differences can do much to interpret the nature of cultural influences on emotional behavior in applied settings, in order to prevent misunderstandings that may have severe consequences. Although little systematic research has been done in this field, we have a sufficient knowledge base to suggest ample ideas that have important practical ramifications as well. Below, I outline briefly how Japanese cultural differences on emotion can have an impact in four applied areas: everyday interactions and social relationships, business, medicine and psychotherapy, and education.

EVERYDAY INTERACTIONS AND SOCIAL RELATIONSHIPS

Our ability to express and perceive emotions accurately across cultures has enormous impact on cross-cultural, social relationships, whether among friends, strangers, intimates, or family members. One of the major obstacles reported by Americans and Japanese alike in cross-cultural interactions has to do with the degree to which they encourage or discourage the open expression of emotions. Unlike the Japanese culture, Western cultures tend to value freer, more truthful expression of self-emotions via nonverbal behavior (Markus & Kitayama, 1991). In Japan, more favorable judgments are attributed to moderated expressivity, reflecting a greater degree of control. When interacting with Japanese people, Americans often express frustration, mistrust, or other negative feelings because the Japanese tend to be reserved. Americans rely on direct, open expression of one's feelings; without it, they feel put down. The Japanese downplay the importance of such directness, and instead prefer to remain reserved. In fact, when interacting with Americans who are just being their usual, open, selves, many Japanese report feeling threatened or overwhelmed, because such direct expression of feelings is usually reserved for other social circumstances. These sorts of situations clearly have the potential for the breakdown of interaction and negative consequences.

The success of social interactions involving people of different cultural backgrounds lies in the recognition of the existence of cultural differences in the expression of emotion and on the patience required to attribute perceived cultural transgressions to culture rather than to the intention of the individual. Cross-cultural research on emotional behaviors and perceptions is well prepared to explain why cultural differences occur, and how they may be overcome to produce successful social outcomes. Programs based on systematic research findings can be developed to teach social skills needed to incorporate such information in designing adequate interventions for participants of different cultural backgrounds. Knowledge, recognition, acceptance, good intentions, and patience are the ingredients to turning a potentially sour social interaction into a rich and rewarding one.

BUSINESS APPLICATIONS

In business, there is a global trend toward more people from diverse backgrounds working together at the domestic level, and more multinational companies operating across cultures at the international level. Japanese companies are increasingly gaining a stronger presence in many economies across the world, including the U.S. Although the challenges and goals of business have not changed, culturally diverse businesses are now even more reliant than before on accurate communication in order to ensure efficiency, productivity, and ultimately, profit. Although verbal communication in intercultural business is usually conducted in one language via interpreters, Japanese cultural differences in emotion and nonverbal behavior cannot be neutralized in this way. Consequently, whether a business relationship with the Japanese will lead to satisfaction, mutual benefit, and profit, or to misunderstanding, resentment, and loss of opportunities depends to a large degree on an understanding of cultural differences in emotional behavior and negotiating style.

One area of consistent frustration on the part of both American and Japanese businesspeople concerns (again) the tension between the open, direct expression of feelings on the American side and the subtle, more reserved approach of the Japanese. When making business decisions, the Japanese tend to take more time, involve more people, and place relatively greater importance on social functions than do Americans. Part of the reason for this is the Japanese wish to make a judgment about their potential partners as people in general, and not merely as business partners. It is not uncommon, for instance, for the Japanese to interact with a potential business partner in many social outings, as well as business, to make this judgment. But in all these encounters the Japanese tend to be reserved, not wishing to mislead their business partners, and to gain as much information as possible. Because Americans are used to quick information dissemination and quick decisions based solely on business merit, and much less on social exchanges, they will often push for an answer and will be frustrated when met by the Japanese reserve.

As a result, there are many instances when a seemingly aloof, neutral response by a Japanese businessperson is interpreted, understandably but incorrectly, by American negotiators as negative. Alternatively, the broad smile of the same Japanese businessperson may be interpreted as positive, when in fact the intention of the overall message is merely one of politeness and compliance during the negotiation. Again, these differences are insurmountable only when the interactants interpret the behaviors of others in their own, ethnocentric way. Patience, good intentions, and acceptance of cultural differences can often lead to successful business outcomes.

MEDICAL, PSYCHOTHERAPEUTIC, AND HEALTH PRACTITIONER RELATIONSHIPS

Japanese cultural differences in emotionality have several consequences relating to health. First of all, culture affects the communication of pain or discomfort, both physical or emotional, in therapeutic relationships. Whereas the American culture fosters direct, overt, verbal communication of pain, the Japanese culture does not. Similar differences exist in reporting symptomatology. Unlike Western cultures, where people verbalize emotional states, particularly of pain or depression, the Japanese tend to hold back in expressing self-emotions verbally and instead communicate through nonverbal behaviors or through indirect symptomatology such as gastrointestinal ailments or lower back pain. Further, it may take longer for Japanese people to seek treatment, because of their wish to minimize expression of pain or other symptomatology.

The Japanese culture also has different values concerning whether and when to seek professional help, especially psychotherapeutic. In the U.S., it has become almost fashionable, particularly in larger urban areas, to have a therapist to whom one can express one's feelings openly. In Japan, this sort of psychotherapeutic relationship is generally frowned upon. One of the reasons for this stems from the general bias against the direct expression of one's emotions in the Japanese culture.

Japanese cultural differences in emotionality can also affect the development of therapeutic rapport in cross-cultural therapeutic relationships. Efficacious psychotherapy depends on the development of positive rapport, and emotional expression and perception contribute greatly to the development or breakdown of rapport, particularly in the initial phases of relationships. Misunderstanding or misinterpretation of underlying emotional states of a Japanese patient by an American physician or psychotherapist are real possibilities given cultural differences in the expression of emotion, which could prevent the development of a working relationship and lead eventually to dropout or noncompliance with treatment regimens.

EMOTIONS IN EDUCATION

Students from Japan flock to the United States every year to further their education. Coming either alone as exchange students, or with their families as part of a business transfer, Japanese students make up a substantial portion of the foreign students in the U.S. Thus, educators need to appreciate and understand the impact of Japanese cultural differences in expressivity on learning.

The American culture encourages its members to question authority, to speak one's mind, and actively to seek out resources for personal growth and learning. Many new educational practices in the U.S. attempt to take advantage of this characteristic in North American students by requiring active participation in the learning process. The Japanese culture discourages students from questioning authority or speaking out in groups; such behavior is considered disrespectful or rude. Instead, it is more proper to sit passively and accept what is being taught in usually a didactic manner.

In the U.S., however, passivity is often misinterpreted by teachers as indicating lack of interest or motivation. Clearly, as a cultural difference, passivity in Japanese students studying in the United States is apt to be misinterpreted. Teachers often express frustration with their

Japanese students because they "don't respond," and Japanese students are dismayed at being expected to "perform"—that is, to speak up in the classroom. If not dealt with adequately, this sort of cultural difference alone can have a harmful effect on the whole educational process. As before, good intentions, patience, and recognition and acceptance of cultural differences on the part of both students and teachers, and families also, are necessary to turn a potentially negative situation into a positive and rewarding one.

Conclusion

One of the main purposes of this book was to gain a better understanding of not only the Japanese culture but also the Japanese people, via the study of human emotion. Emotion is a universal concept, and because it is universal to all human beings, it gives us a common basis by which we can further our attempts to study, understand, and interact with people of different cultures. Although the Japanese people and culture have come under scrutiny many times, most attempts at understanding have relied on analyses of macrolevel constructs such as society or culture. The study of human emotions gives us some common ground to understand the Japanese as people, and the social and cultural forces that affect them as individuals.

This book has presented current information concerning the feelings and emotions of the Japanese as uncovered in research on the various components of emotion in Japan. Chapter 2 explained how the facial expressions of emotion of the Japanese are biologically innate and panculturally similar to people of other cultures. Chapter 3 discussed how the Japanese learn to modify their use of the universal expressions by following cultural display rules. Chapter 4 discussed how the Japanese are both similar to and different from people of other cultures in their subjective experience of emotion, including the frequency, intensity, and control of self-reported emotions, as well as nonverbal reactions and physiological sensations. Chapter 5 discussed the antecedents and elicitors of emotion in Japan, and how the Japanese evaluate those antecedents. Chapter 6 described our current knowledge of Japanese cultural similarities and differences in the perception of emotion, including judgments of what kinds of emotions are being expressed in others, and how strongly. Chapter 7 discussed the language of emotion, examining how the Japanese mold their emotional experiences via similarities and differences to the emotion lexicons of other cultures. Finally, Chapter 8 discussed some ways by which our theoretical understanding of Japanese cultural similarities and differences could be furthered by using meaningful dimensions of cultural variability known as individualism-collectivism and status differentiation.

The information presented in this volume was not based solely on personal observation or experiential anecdote. Rather, it was distilled from many cross-cultural studies of human emotion in Japan, much of it generated from our own laboratory and already published in the scientific journals. By basing our information on evidence documented by research conducted according to acceptable scientific standards and care, I have hoped to bridge the gap between academic research on the one hand and the interested, educated, and informed public on the other. By relying on the scientific process for our knowledge base, I have sought to raise our discussions of this important topic from the level of observation and anecdote to documented, scientific evidence culled from systematic cross-cultural research.

My goal has not been to set aside the previous literature that has contributed to our great understanding of Japanese culture, but to add to it. As most informed readers of Japanese society and culture are aware, there are many resources available on the Japanese culture, society, and people, many of them well-known standards in this area, including the works by Ruth Benedict, Takeo Doi, Nakane Chie, Takie Sugiyama Lebra, Edwin Reischauer, and so on. These authors, and many others, have all contributed to an important, and continually growing, literature on the Japanese culture and people. Some of this has been based on anthropological research methods using observations and ethnography, or on analyses of social structure. Some works have analyzed language usages; others have been based in observations of clinical patients, or on astute observations and personal anecdote.

Though variously directed, nearly all these studies have at least in a secondary way, paid some attention to the exploration of Japanese emotions in some shape or form—guilt vs. shame, for example, or *amae*. A number of scholars have examined morality and moral reasoning (e.g., DeVos, Lebra), which are closely related to emotion. Regardless of the approach and the main topic of focus, these previous works have all contributed in important ways to our understanding, knowledge, and interest in Japan and the Japanese. I can only sincerely hope that the information provided in this book, which is based on cross-cultural, psychological research on human emotions in Japan, has given yet another glimpse into the private world of emotions in the Japanese culture. If this book stimulates a better understanding of the complexity of emotions in Japan, a better appreciation of the impact of cultural and social forces in the molding of emotion, and a deeper sense of respect for the Japanese as people who need to deal with the emotional results of one of the most influential and taxing of world cultures, then it will have achieved its goal.

References Cited

References Cited

Allport, F. (1924). *Social psychology*. Boston: Houghton Mifflin.

Asch, S. E. (1952). *Social psychology*. Englewood Cliffs, NJ: Prentice-Hall.

Averill, J. R. (1975). A constructivist view of emotion. In R. Plutchik and H. Kellerman (Eds.), *Theories of emotion*. San Diego: Academic Press.

Bard, P. (1934). On emotional expression after decortication with some remarks on certain theoretical views, Parts I and II. *Psychological Review, 41*, 309–329, 424–449.

Barnlund, D. C. (1975). *Public and private self in Japan and the United States: Communicative styles of two cultures*. Tokyo: Simul Press.

Benedict, R. (1946). *The crysanthemum and the sword: Patterns of Japanese culture*. Boston: Houghton Mifflin.

Birdwhistell, R. L. (1970). *Kinesics and context*. Philadelphia: University of Pennsylvania Press.

Blumberg, S. H., Solomon, G. E., & Perloe, S. I. (1981). *Display rules and the facial communication of emotion*. Unpublished manuscript, Haverford College.

Bradshaw, D. L., Miyake, K., Campos, J., Kanaya, Y., & Usui. H. (1990). *Predictors of and maternal response to Japanese toddlers' expressions of negative affect in control interactions*. Paper presented at the Bi-Annual Meetings of the International Society for Research on Emotions, Rutgers University.

Brandt, M. E., & Boucher, J. D. (1986). Concepts of depression in emotion lexicons of eight cultures. *International Journal of Intercultural Relations, 10*, 321–346.

Brewer, M. B., & Kramer, R. M. (1985). The psychology of intergroup attitudes and behavior. *Annual Review of Psychology, 36,* 219–243.

Buck, (1984). *The communication of emotion.* New York: Guilford Press.

Camras, L. (1985). The socialization of affect communication. In M. Lewis and C. Saarni (Eds.), *The socialization of emotions.* New York: Plenum Press.

Camras, L., Campos, J., Oster, H., & Bradshaw, D. (1990). *Facial responses of American and Japanese infants to putative elicitors of anger.* Paper presented at the Bi-Annual Meetings of the International Society for Research on Emotions, Rutgers University.

Cannon, W. B. (1927). The James-Lange theory of emotions: A critical examination and an alternative theory. *American Journal of Psychology, 39,* 106–124.

Chan, D. W. (1990). The meaning of depression: Chinese word associations. *Psychologia, 33,* 191–196.

Cole, P. M. (1985). Display rules and the socialization of affective displays. In G. Zivin (Ed.), *The development of expressive behavior.* New York: Academic Press.

Condon, J. (1984). *With respect to the Japanese: A guide for Americans.* Yarmouth, ME: Intercultural Press.

Condon, J., & Saito, M. (Eds.). (1974). *Intercultural encounter with Japan: The proceedings of the 1972 conference on intercultural communication.* Tokyo: Simul.

Darwin, C. (1872). *The expression of emotions in man and animals.* New York: Philosophical Library.

De Vos, G. (1973). *Socialization for achievement: Essays on the cultural psychology of the Japanese.* Berkeley: University of California Press.

De Vos, G. (1986). The relation of guilt toward parents to achievement and arranged marriage among the Japanese. In T. S. Lebra and W. P. Lebra (Eds.), *Japanese culture and behavior: Selected readings.* Honolulu: University of Hawaii Press.

Dickey, R., & Knower, F. H. (1941). A note on some ethnological differences in recognition of simulated expressions of the emotions. *American Journal of Sociology, 47,* 190–193.

Doi, T. (1973). *The anatomy of dependence.* Tokyo: Kodansha.

Doi, T. (1985). *The anatomy of self.* Tokyo: Kodansha.

Dore, R. P. (1967). Mobility, equality, and individuation in modern Japan. In R. P. Dore (Ed.), *Aspects of social change in modern Japan.* Princeton, NJ: Princeton University Press.

Ekman, P. (1972). Universals and cultural differences in facial expressions of emotion. In J. Cole (Ed.), *Nebraska symposium of motivation, 1971* (Vol. 19). Lincoln: University of Nebraska Press.

Ekman, P. (1973). *Darwin and facial expression.* New York: Academic Press.

Ekman, P. (1978). Facial signs: Facts, fantasies, and possibilities. In T. Sebeok (Ed.), *Sight, sound, and sense.* Bloomington: Indiana University Press.

Ekman, P. (1985). *Telling lies.* New York: Norton.

Ekman, P. (1994). Strong evidence for universals in facial expressions: A reply to Russell's mistaken critique. *Psychological Bulletin, 115,* 268–287.

Ekman, P., Davidson, R., & Friesen, W. (1990). The Duchenne smile: Emotional expression and brain physiology II. *Journal of Personality and Social Psychology, 58,* 342–353.

Ekman, P., & Friesen, W. V. (1969). The repertoire of nonverbal behavior—Categories, origins, usage, and coding. *Semiotica, 1,* 49–98.

Ekman, P., & Friesen, W. V. (1971). Constants across cultures in the face and emotion. *Journal of Personality and Social Psychology, 17,* 124–129.

Ekman, P., & Freisen, W. V. (1975). *Unmasking the face.* Englewood Cliffs, NJ: Prentice-Hall.

Ekman, P., & Friesen, W. V. (1978). *The facial action coding system (FACS).* Palo Alto, CA: Consulting Psychologists Press.

Ekman, P., & Friesen, W. (1982). Felt, false, and miserable smiles. *Journal of Nonverbal Behavior, 6,* 238–252.

Ekman, P., & Friesen, W. (1986). A new pan-cultural expression of emotion. *Motivation and Emotion, 10,* 159–168.

Ekman, P., Friesen, W. V., & Ellsworth, P. (1972). *Emotion in the human face.* New York: Pergamon.

Ekman, P., Friesen, W. V., O'Sullivan, M., Chan, A. Diacoyanni-Tarlatzis, I., Heider, K., Krause, R., LeCompte, W. A., Pitcairn, T. Ricci-Bitti, P. E., Scherer, K., Tomita, M., & Tzavaras, A. (1987). Universals and cultural differences in the judgments of facial expressions of emotion. *Journal of Personality and Social Psychology, 53,* 712–717.

Ekman, P., & Heider, K. (1988). The universality of a contempt expression: A replication. *Motivation and Emotion, 12,* 303–308.

Ekman, P., Sorenson, E. R., & Friesen, W. V. (1969). Pan-cultural elements in facial displays of emotions. *Science, 164,* 86–88.

Friesen, W. V. (1972). *Cultural differences in facial expressions in a social situation: An experimental test of the concept of display rules.* Unpublished doctoral dissertation, University of California, San Francisco.

Gerber, E. (1975). *The cultural patterning of emotions in Samoa.* Unpublished doctoral dissertation, University of California, San Diego.

Gudykunst, W. B. (1991). *Bridging differences: Effective intergroup communication.* Newbury Park, CA: Sage.

Gudykunst, W. B., & Nishida, T. (1994). *Bridging Japanese/North American differences.* Newbury Park, CA: Sage.

Gudykunst, W. B., & Ting-Toomey, S. (1988). Culture and affective communication. *American Behavioral Scientist, 31*, 384–400.

Hall, E. T. (1976). *Beyond culture.* New York: Doubleday.

Hamaguchi, E., & Kumon, S. (Eds.). (1982). *Nihonteki shūdan shugi* (Japanese collectivism). Tokyo: Yuhikaku Press.

Hearn, L. (1894). *Glimpses of unfamiliar Japan.* Boston: Houghton Mifflin.

Hiatt, L. R. (1978). Classification of the emotions. In L. R. Hiatt (Ed.), *Australian aboriginal concepts.* Princeton, NJ: Humanities Press.

Hofstede, G. (1980). *Culture's consequences.* Beverly Hills, CA: Sage.

Hofstede, G. (1983). Dimensions of national cultures in fifty countries and three regions. In J. Deregowski, S. Dziurawiec, & R. Annis (Eds.), *Expiscations in cross-cultural psychology.* Lisse, Denmark-Swets & Zeitlinger.

Howell, S. (1981). Rules not words. In P. Heelas and A. Lock (Eds.), *Indigenous psychologies: The anthropology of the self.* San Diego: Academic Press.

Imada, H. (1989). Cross-language comparisons of emotional terms with special reference to the concept of anxiety. *Japanese Psychological Research, 31*, 10–19.

Imada, H., Araki, M., & Kujime, Y. (1991). *Comparisons of concepts of anxiety, fear, and depression in English and Japanese languages.* Unpublished manuscript, Kawnsei Gakuin University, Department of Psychology, Hyogo, Japan.

Ishida, E. (1986). A culture of love and hate. In T. S. Lebra and W. P. Lebra (Eds.), *Japanese culture and behavior: Selected readings.* Honolulu: University of Hawaii Press.

Izard, C. E. (1971). *The face of emotion.* New York: Appleton-Century-Crofts.

Kemper, T. (1978). *A social interactional theory of emotions.* New York: Wiley.

Kilbride, J. E., & Yarczower, M. (1980). Recognition and imitation of facial expressions: A cross-cultural comparison between Zambia and the United States. *Journal of Cross-Cultural Psychology, 11*, 281–296.

Kleck, R. E., Vaughan, R. C., Cartwright-Smith, J., Vaughan, K. B., Colby, C., & Lanzetta, J. (1976). Effects of being observed in expressive, subjective, and physiological reactions to painful stimuli. *Journal of Personality and Social Psychology, 34*, 1211–1218.

Kluckholn, F., & Strodbeck, F. (1961). *Variations in value orientations.* Evanston, IL: Row, Peterson.

Kraut, R. E. (1982). Social presence, facial feedback, and emotion. *Journal of Personality and Social Psychology, 42*, 853–863.

LaBarre, W. (1947). The cultural basis of emotions and gestures. *Journal of Personality, 16,* 49–68.

LaBarre, W. (1962). *Paralanguage, kinesics, and cultural anthropology. Report for the Interdisciplinary Work Conference on Paralanguage and Kinesics.* Bloomington: Indiana University Research Center in Anthropology, Folklore, and Linguistics.

Laird, J. (1984). The real role of facial response in the experience of emotion: A reply to Tourangeau and Ellsworth and others. *Journal of Personality and Social Psychology, 47,* 909–917.

Lange, C. G., & James, W. (1922). *The emotions.* Baltimore: Williams and Wilkins.

Lanham, B. B. (1986). Ethics and moral precepts taught in schools in Japan and the United States. In T. S. Lebra and W. P. Lebra (Eds.), *Japanese culture and behavior: Selected readings.* Honolulu: University of Hawaii Press.

Lazarus, R. S. (1966). *Psychological stress and the coping process.* New York: McGraw-Hill.

Lazarus, R. S. (1991). *Emotion and adaptation.* New York: Oxford University Press.

Lebra, T. S. (1976). *Japanese patterns of behavior.* Honolulu: University of Hawaii Press.

Lebra, T. S. (1986). Compensative justice and moral investment among Japanese, Chinese, and Koreans. In T. S. Lebra and W. P. Lebra (Eds.), *Japanese culture and behavior: Selected readings.* Honolulu: University of Hawaii Press.

Leff, J. (1973). Culture and the differentiation of emotional states. *British Journal of Psychiatry, 123,* 299–306.

Leventhal, H. (1984). In K. R. Scherer and P. Ekman (Eds.), *Approaches to emotion.* Hillsdale, NJ: Erlbaum.

Levy, R. I. (1973). *Tahitians.* Chicago: University of Chicago Press.

Levy, R. I. (1984). The emotions in comparative perspective. In K. R. Scherer and P. Ekman (Eds.), *Approaches to emotion.* Hillsdale, NJ: Erlbaum.

Lutz, C. (1982). The domain of emotion words in Ifaluk. *American Ethnologist, 9,* 113–128.

Lutz, C. (1983). Parental goals, ethnopsychology, and the development of emotional meaning. *Ethos, 11,* 246–262.

Malatesta, C. Z., & Haviland, J. M. (1985). Signals, symbols, and socialization. The modification of emotional expression in human development. In M. Lewis and C. Saarni (Eds.), *The socialization of emotions.* New York: Plenum Press.

Markus, H. R., & Kitayama, S. (1991). Culture and the self: Implications for cognition, emotion, and motivation. *Psychological Review, 98*, 224–253.

Marmot, M. G., & Syme, S. L. (1976). Acculturation and coronary heart disease in Japanese-Americans. *American Journal of Epidemiology, 104*, 225–247.

Matsumoto, D. (1986). *Cross-cultural communication of emotion.* Unpublished doctoral dissertation, University of California, Berkeley.

Matsumoto, D. (1987). On the role of facial response in the experience of emotion: Methodological issues and a meta analysis. *Journal of Personality and Social Psychology, 52*, 769–774.

Matsumoto, D. (1989a). Cultural influences on the perception of emotion. *Journal of Cross-Cultural Psychology, 20*, 92–105.

Matsumoto, D. (1989b). Face, culture, and judgments of anger and fear: Do the eyes have it? *Journal of Nonverbal Behavior, 13*, 171–188.

Matsumoto, D. (1990). Cultural similarities and differences in display rules. *Motivation and Emotions, 14*, 195–214.

Matsumoto, D. (1991). Cultural influences on facial expressions of emotion. *Southern Communication Journal, 56*, 128–137.

Matsumoto, D. (1992a). American-Japanese cultural differences in the recognition of universal facial expressions. *Journal of Cross-Cultural Psychology, 23*, 72–84.

Matsumoto, D. (1992b). More evidence for the universality of a contempt expression. *Motivation and Emotion, 16*, 363–368.

Matsumoto, D., & Ekman, P. (1988). *Japanese and Caucasian Facial Expressions of Emotion (JACFEE) and Neutral Faces (JACNeuF).* [Slides]. Intercultural and Emotional Research Laboratory, Department of Psychology, San Francisco State University.

Matsumoto, D., & Ekman, P. (1989). American-Japanese cultural differences in intensity ratings of facial expressions of emotion. *Motivation and Emotion, 13*, 143–157.

Matsumoto, D., & Hearn, V. (1991). *Culture and emotion: Display rule differences between the United States, Poland, and Hungary.* Manuscript submitted for publication.

Matsumoto, D., and Kishimoto, H. (1983). Developmental characteristics in judgments of emotion from nonverbal vocal cues. *International Journal of Intercultural Relations, 7*, 415–424.

Matsumoto, D., & Kudoh, T. (1993). American-Japanese cultural differences in attributions of personality based on smiles. *Journal of Nonverbal Behavior, 17*, 231–243.

Matsumoto, D., Kudoh, T., Scherer, K., & Wallbott, H. (1988). Emotion antecedents and reactions in the US and Japan. *Journal of Cross-Cultural Psychology, 19,* 267–286.

Matsumoto, D., Kudoh, T., & Takeuchi, S. (1995). *Psychology in Japan: A case for constructive skepticism of western psychology and research.* Manuscript submitted for publication.

Matsumoto, D., Wallbott, H., & Scherer, K. (1989). Emotion and intercultural communication. In W. Gudykunst and M. Asante (Eds.), *Handbook of Intercultural and International Communication.* Beverly Hills, CA: Sage.

Matsumoto, D., Wallbott, H., & Scherer, K. R. (in prep.). *Emotion antecedents and reactions across cultures: A study of 30 countries on five continents.*

Matsumoto, D., Weissman, M., Preston, K., & Brown, B. (1993) *Context-specific measurement of individualism-collectivism on the individual level: The IC Assessment Inventory (ICAI).* Manuscript currently submitted for publication.

Matsuyama, Y., Hama, H., Kawamura, Y., & Mine, H. (1978). An analysis of emotion words. *Japanese Journal of Psychology, 49,* 229–232.

Mauro, R., Sato, K., & Tucker, J. (1992). The role of appraisal in human emotions: A cross-cultural study. *Journal of Personality and Social Psychology, 62,* 301–317.

Mead, M. (1967). *Cooperation and competition among primitive people.* Boston: Beacon.

Messick, D. M., & Mackie, D. M. (1989). Intergroup relations. *Annual Review of Psychology, 40,* 45–81.

Michalson, L., & Lewis, M. (1985). What do children know about emotions and when do they know it? In M. Lewis and C. Saarni (Eds.), *The socialization of emotions.* New York: Plenum Press.

Moeran, B. (1986). Individual, group, and seishin: Japan's internal cultural debate. In T. S. Lebra and W. P. Lebra (Eds.), *Japanese culture and behavior: Selected readings.* Honolulu: University of Hawaii Press.

Mulder, M. (1976). Reduction of power differences in practice: The power distance reduction theory and its applications. In G. Hofstede and M. S. Kassem (Eds.), *European contributions to organize theory.* Assen, Netherlands: Van Gorcum.

Mulder, M. (1977). *The daily power game.* Leyden: Martinus.

Myers, F. R. (1979). Emotions and the self: A theory of personhood and political order among Pintupi aborigines. *Ethos, 7,* 343–370.

Nakane, C. (1970). *Japanese society.* Berkeley: University of California Press.

Oster, H. (1990). *Affectively negative facial expressions in Japanese and*

American infants. Paper presented at the Bi-Annual Meetings of the International Society for Research on Emotions, Rutgers University.

Pelto, P. J. (1968). The differences between "tight" and "loose" societies. *Trans-Action, April*, 37–40.

Pelzel, J. C. (1986). Human nature in the Japanese myths. In T. S. Lebra and W. P. Lebra (Eds.), *Japanese culture and behavior: Selected readings*. Honolulu: University of Hawaii Press.

Piers, G., & Singer, M. B. (1953). *Shame and guilt: A psychoanalytic and a cultural study*. Springfield, IL: W. W. Norton.

Reischauer, E. O. (1988). *The Japanese today: Change and continuity*. Cambridge, MA: Harvard University Press.

Riesman, P. (1977). *Freedom in Fulani social life: An introspective ethnography*. Chicago: University of Chicago Press.

Russell, J. A. (1983). Pancultural aspects of human conceptual organization of emotions. *Journal of Personality and Social Psychology, 45*, 1281–1288.

Russell, J. A. (1991). Culture and the categorization of emotions. *Psychological Bulletin, 110*, 426–450.

Saarni, C. (1985). Indirect process in affect socialization. In M. Lewis and C. Saarni (Eds.), *The socialization of emotions*. New York: Plenum Press.

Sakuta, K. (1967). *Haji no bunka saikō* (Shame culture re-examined). Tokyo: Chikuma Shobo.

Schachter, S., & Singer, J. (1962). Cognitive, social, and physiological determinants of emotional state. *Psychological Review, 69*, 379–399.

Scherer, K. R. (1984). On the nature and function of emotion. In K. R. Scherer and P. Ekman (Eds.), *Approaches to emotion*. Hillsdale, NJ: Erlbaum.

Scherer, K., Matsumoto, D., Wallbott, H., & Kudoh, T. (1988). Emotional experience in cultural context: A comparison between Europe, Japan, and the USA. In K. Scherer (Ed.), *Facets of emotion: Recent research*. Hillsdale, NJ: Erlbaum.

Scherer, K. R., Wallbott, H., & Summerfield, A. (1986). *Experiencing emotion: A cross-cultural study*. Cambridge: Cambridge University Press.

Stevenson, H., Lee, S., & Stigler, J. (1986a). Digit memory in Chinese and English: Evidence for temporarily limited store. *Cognition, 23*, 1–20.

Stevenson, H., Lee, S., & Stigler, J. (1986b). Mathematics achievement of Chinese, Japanese, and American children. *Science, 231*, 693–698.

Suzuki, T. (1973). *Kotoba to bunka* (Japanese and the Japanese: Words in culture). Tokyo: Iwanami Shoten.

Suzuki, T. (1986). Language and behavior in Japan: The conceptualization of personal relations. In T. S. Lebra and W. P. Lebra (Eds.), *Japanese culture and behavior: Selected readings*. Honolulu: University of Hawaii Press.

Tajfel, H. (1982). Social psychology of intergroup relations. *Annual Review of Psychology, 33*, 1–39.

Tanaka-Matsumi, J., & Marsella, A. (1976). Cross-cultural variations in the phenomenological experience of depression: I. Word association studies. *Journal of Cross-Cultural Psychology, 7*, 379–396.

Tanaka-Matsumi, J., & Marsella, A. (1977). *Ethnocultural variations in the subjective experience of depression: Semantic differential.* Unpublished manuscript, University of Hawaii, Department of Psychology.

Tomkins, S. (1962). *Affect, imagery, consciousness* (Vol 1). New York: Springer-Verlag.

Tomkins, S. (1963). *Affect, imagery, consciousness* (Vol 2). New York: Springer-Verlag.

Tomkins, S. (1984). Affect theory. In K. S. Scherer and P. Ekman (Eds.), *Approaches to emotion.* Hillsdale, NJ: Erlbaum.

Triandis, H. (1972). *The analysis of subjective culture.* New York: Wiley.

Triandis, H. C. (1992). *Individualism-collectivism as a cultural syndrome.* Paper presented at the Annual Meeting of the Society for Cross-Cultural Research, Santa Fe, New Mexico.

Triandis, H. C., Bontempo, R., Villareal, M. J., Asai, M., & Lucca, N. (1988). Individualism and collectivism: Cross-cultural perspectives on self-ingroup relationships. *Journal of Personality and Social Psychology, 54*, 323–338.

Triandis, H. C., & Lambert, W. W. (1958). A restatement and test of Schlosberg's theory of emotion with two kinds of subjects from Greece. *Journal of Abnormal and Social Psychology, 56*, 321–328.

Vinacke, W. E. (1949). The judgment of facial expressions by three national-racial groups in Hawaii: I. Caucasian faces. *Journal of Personality, 17*, 407–429.

Vinacke, W. E., & Fong, R. W. (1955). The judgment of facial expressions by three national-racial groups in Hawaii: II. Oriental faces. *Journal of Social Psychology, 41*, 184–195.

Vogel, E. (1963). *Japan's new middle class: The salary man and his family in a Tokyo suburb.* Berkeley: University of California Press.

Wallbott, H. G., & Scherer, K. R. (1986). How universal and specific is emotional experience? Evidence from 27 countries on five continents. *Social Science Information, 25*, 763–796.

Wallbott, H. G., & Scherer, K. R. (1988). Emotion and economic development—Data and speculations concerning the relationship between emotional experience and socio-economic factors. *European Journal of Social Psychology, 18*, 267–273.

White, G. M. (1980). Conceptual universals in interpersonal language. *American Anthropologist, 82*, 752–781.

Winton, W. (1986). The role of facial response in self-reports of emotion: A critique of Laird. *Journal of Personality and Social Psychology, 50,* 808–812.

Yarczower, M., & Daruns, I. (1982). Social inhibition of spontaneous facial expressions in children. *Journal of Personality and Social Psychology, 43,* 831–837.

Yarczower, M., Kilbride, J. E., & Hill, L. A. (1979). Imitation and inhibition of facial expression. *Developmental Psychology, 15,* 453–454.

Yoshida, M., Kinase, R., Kurokawa, J., & Yashiro, S. (1970). Multidimensional scaling of emotion. *Japanese Psychological Research, 12,* 45–61.

Zajonc, R. B. (1980). Feeling and thinking: Preferences need no inferences. *American Psychologist, 35,* 151–175.

Index

Library of Congress Cataloging-in-Publication Data

Matsumoto, David
    Unmasking Japan : myths and realities about the emotions of the
Japanese / David Matsumoto.
       p.   cm.
    Includes bibliographical references and index.
    ISBN 0-8047-2719-8 (cloth : alk. paper).
    1. Japanese—Psychology.   2. National characteristics—Japanese.
    3. Emotions—Cross-cultural studies.   I. Title.
    DS830.M345 1996
    152.4'0942—dc20   96-16555
                                                  CIP

Original Printing 1996
Last figure below indicates year of this printing:
05   04   03   02   01   00   99   98   97   96